847489

728.3 Schram, Joseph F.
SCH

Successful
children's rooms

DATE			

⌂ SUCCESSFUL CHILDREN'S ROOMS

⌂ SUCCESSFUL CHILDREN'S ROOMS

Joseph F. Schram

Manufactured in the United States of America

Edited by Shirley M. Horowitz

Design by Carey Jean Ferchland

Cover photo courtesy of Armstrong Cork Company

Current Printing (last digit)
10   9   8   7   6   5   4   3   2   1

Structures Publishing Co.
Box 1002, Farmington, Mich. 48024

Library of Congress Cataloging in Publication Data

Schram, Joseph F.
    Successful children's rooms.

    Includes index.
    1. Children's rooms. 2. Interior decoration.
I. Title.
NK2117.C4S35   728.3   79-11967
ISBN 0-912336-85-4
ISBN 0-912336-86-2 pbk.

Contents

Plastics play an important role in this attic hideaway. The lightweight furniture, storage-bunk, and wall-hung play table free up extra space in a small room. The washable wallcoverings are strippable and vinyl coated. (Photo courtesy of Imperial Wallcoverings)

Introduction

The American homebuyer over the past 25 years has been offered a glittering array of new products, materials and designs in single-family homes. Through all of this, perhaps the least consideration has been given to the child's role in a home. Think for a moment of the model homes you have visited, and you will quickly recall that the selling emphasis has always been placed on the beautiful modern kitchen, the lavish bathroom, and the adult-oriented master bedroom suite "where you can close the door and get away from the children". Few in the housing industry have unleashed their talents in the direction of child's spaces in the home. They have left you to try to fit the necessary furniture, toys, etc. into the child's room, which is generally the smallest.

Educators stress that parents can create better environments for their children at home by encouraging their independence. This may even begin with placing food and drink on a low shelf in the refrigerator so that when a young child wants food he can help himself. It continues as we arrange the home environment in such a way that children can control themselves and their activities instead of requiring constant adult assistance.

Successful Children's Rooms will assist you in first understanding the very basics of planning and building home spaces for children, and then making use of countless ideas that will help you provide your children with their own space in the family home.

There is no better person than you to determine exactly what your children need in your home, since you are aware of their likes and dislikes, their needs, their goals and most importantly, their daily routines. With the material that follows you should be able to match each child to a more pleasant surrounding, one he or she can be comfortable in.

Builders and designers will tell you without reservation that there is a demand today for more practical space division of the home. Both children and adults are asking for more separation to pursue separate past-times in leisure hours. Add to this demand the fact that today's children have become loaded with their own special possessions—their abundant clothes, elaborate and enormous toys, and educational equipment—and you will see why it's difficult to get two or three fully-equipped children into just one bedroom.

Interior designer Arthur Burke, ASID, created this bedroom for a thirteen-year-old girl, using a blue and red floral fabric to set the mood. The canopied bed was easily created with a length of fabric and dowels suspended from the ceiling. Burke repeated the fabric on closet doors and on the walls where the reversed wainscoting features richly grained paneling. (Photo courtesy of Masonite Corporation)

1
The Child's Bedroom

Of all the areas within the home that can be set apart for our youngsters—whether infant, child, or teen—the bedroom offers the most opportunities for contribution to the young person's development, personality, growth, and self-expression. The knowledge that he or she possesses his own territorial space can positively affect emotional outlook.

Furniture designers who in the past have designed the child's bedroom have for the most part merely come up with scaled-down adult rooms. Interior designers, and probably rightly so in economic terms, have devoted their efforts to the master bedroom (where more expensive furniture can be utilized) while the children's rooms accepted hand-me-down furniture from early days of marriage, or bargains from a variety of locations. However, far-thinking designers and childhood experts are showing increasing signs of departing from this tradition in order to create children's rooms that are oriented more toward the needs of the occupants.

Noted West Coast Designer Marlene Grant, for example, firmly believes the child's bedroom should be dramatically changed from what adults inhabit to what children find comfortable during their three age cycles: birth to seven years, eight through twelve years, and teenage to departure from the parents' home. Mrs. Grant speaks for a growing number of designers who believe placing a baby in a 10' x 12' room with an 8-foot ceiling and a crib as large as a single adult bed unnecessarily creates fear in the child. She rightly asks how an adult would feel sleeping in the middle of a gymnasium.

"CHILD LEVEL"

Studies conducted at Stanford University's renowned Bing Nursery School clearly illustrate that "child level" furnishings create a better place to grow and learn. High chairs (dangerous because of the possible damage when an infant falls out), play pens and cribs have been found to be "restraining devices" that increase the child's dependency on adults. For both physical and mental health reasons, the answer appears to be better-scaled furniture and surroundings. The room itself can be allocated into zones to include sleep areas, storage and play space.

Just the room itself, without furnishings, presents a totally different environment to a child than to an adult. The ceilings seem so high that they are almost out of sight; yet these same ceilings serve as the background for the child when looking up at other children and at adults. Bedrooms and playrooms can become "children's rooms" by lowering the ceilings, adding lofts, using scaled-down furniture, replacing the forbidding floor-to-ceiling door with Dutch-style doors, careful color selection for specific sections of the room, and placement of pillows and shelves at "child level." Ceilings which normally measure 8 feet in height can easily be lowered to a more proportionate 5 or 6 feet for children by attaching parachutes or double sheets around the walls and creating a new, soft, lower ceiling. At the same time, a comfortable area that has been furnished with pillows and screened off from the rest of the room can effectively communicate a sense of passivity and quiet to children that will encourage them to relax at rest time.

Many child experts believe that children should be taught to recognize sleepiness and should be encouraged to initiate their own naps. In safe and accessible environments, children can learn to initiate behavior without constantly seeking help or adult approval. These same experts believe parents need to stop doing everything so their children will learn to judge accurately for themselves.

Converting a Sun Porch into a Bedroom

Converting a combination sun porch and summer bedroom in an older home to an attractive year-round bedroom can be carried out successfully and inexpensively if the homeowner keeps an open mind to designer recommendations, has the patience and ability to do some of the work himself, and carefully evaluates costs of alternative materials. New York interior designer Penny Hallock Lehman, ASID, worked with a New Jersey family on their home, built in 1917. No improvements had been made in 25 years. Ms. Lehman's clients agreed that the sun porch had several architectural problems, and that creative use of paneling and wallcovering would help correct them. A french door was selected to complement the only mandatory requirement for the room — a canopy bed for the family's pre-teen daughter. Structural problems were tackled by the entire family. Rotted wood was torn out, primarily from around the windows. Outside shingles that were nailed to one side were removed. Two windows were eliminated and the outside closure was patched with materials on hand to match the rest of the house. Everything else was stripped down to the bare wood. Rough surfaces left by removing the shingles, plus the room's lack of insulation, led to the decision to panel wherever possible. Insulation was added, then prefinished hardboard paneling reflecting a Country French design was installed. Each panel has three long, narrow panel sections 16 in. wide. This modular design was utilized effectively by cutting the panels lengthwise and installing the 16-in. sections between two windows along one wall, and between a window and two shadowboxes that were built into the adjoining wall. A patterned wallcovering was used on the ceiling, valances and lower walls. Cutouts from the wallcovering were glued to the window shades to enhance the pattern. Netting and simple uprights created the four-poster canopy effect at a much lower cost. Carpeting, new lighting and a combination of new and old furniture completed the project.

Before

After

A wood feature wall in this youngster's room includes a handy storage unit with adjustable shelves that can be rearranged to suit the changing needs of your child. (Photo courtesy of Western Wood Products Assn.)

Basics for Smaller Sizing

In the course of researching this book, I found very few studies related to bedroom planning and, in almost all instances, encountered the same basics as set forth by the government in HUD's Minimum Property Standards. Among these basics are the following requirements related to children's rooms:

- a minimum "least" wall length of 8 feet, with greater length desirable for better furniture placement;
- a minimum 32-inch-wide entry door at standard 80 inch height;
- at least one outside window with sill height no more than 4 feet from the floor, the openable area of window not less than 5 square feet with no dimension less than 22 inches;
- a minimum 36-inch closet rod length for one-person secondary bedroom and 60-inch rod length for a two-person room.

The other two most important dimensions to keep in mind in planning any bedroom arrangement (whether child or adult) are 28 inches and 40 inches. Both dimensions relate specifically to bed placement, with the lesser dimension being the distance between the bed and a wall; the 40 inches is the space needed between the foot of the bed and other side of the bed facing the opposite wall, furniture or closet front. The 28-inch dimension is also the distance recommended between twin beds.

Most bedrooms in modern homes have been designed with the entry door located no more than 24 inches from the corner of the room in order to avoid interference with furniture. Keep in mind that in-swinging doors require a minimum 32-inch arc space from hinged jamb to latch jamb. When the door is placed 24 inches from the room corner, a special hinge stop can be used to limit the door swing and to permit furniture placement in that two-foot area.

A later chapter deals specifically with children's

Designed as a "total environment" unit for two children, this GAF "Super System" features two bunk beds, a desk/shelf area, and a long storage area for skis, etc. Tools, materials and details are featured on page 25, Chapter 2. (Photo courtesy of GAF Corporation)

furniture, but your planning will most certainly involve the following minimum mattress sizes:

Crib	27 x 48 inches
Twin	39 x 75 inches
Full	54 x 75 inches
Long Twin	39 x 80 inches
Long Full	54 x 80 inches

CHILD-ORIENTED ADAPTATIONS

Younger Years

The use of Dutch doors enables parents to close the lower section so the child feels he is on his own, while the top half can be left open so that parents can unobtrusively check in frequently.

Carpeted cylinders and platforms are excellent for a young child's room. These elements can help identify a play section or, equipped with a "pad," signal a sleep area. Boxes and cubicles into which children may shove their toys will more readily prompt cleanup than will conventional dressers and drawers.

Designer Grant stresses the use of the "blue family" on the color wheel for the sleep section of a young child's room, and shuns wild graphics. Likewise, she recommends the use of smooth carpet squares to provide a reassuring warm surface, as well as furniture blocks and blinds which permit full to total blockout of daylight. She and others point to allergy problems which can occur with shag carpeting, draperies, and wood blinds that gather dust.

As the child reaches six or seven years of age, parents are much more aware of the interests of the youngster and can help to direct him or her in the selection of bedroom furnishings. Again, programming the room for varied activities is highly desirable. The child's interests, whether animals, camping, athletics, or other topics, should be drawn upon when selecting wallcoverings. Again, it should be

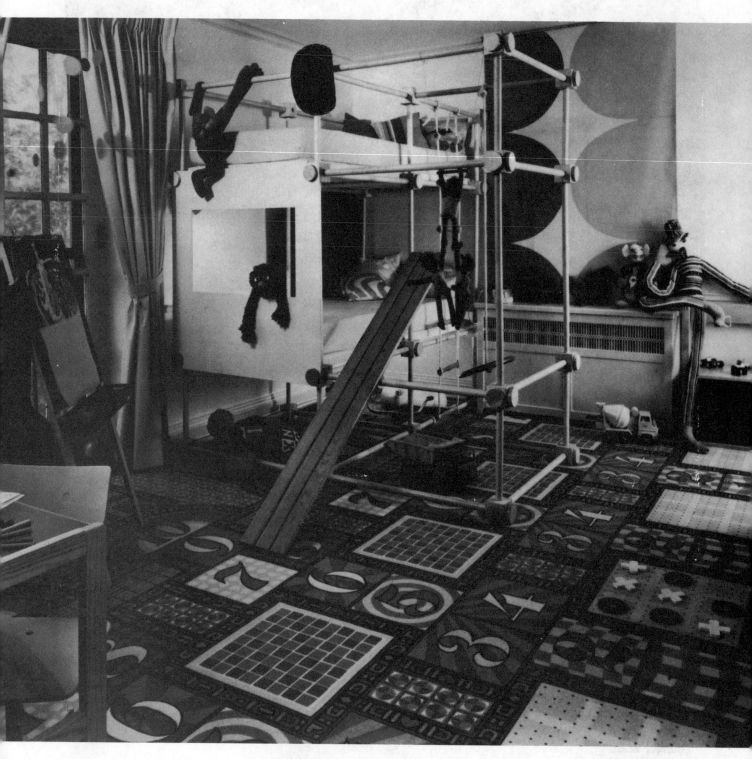

Home-assembled furniture adds considerably to the enjoyment of a child's room. Units such as these save valuable floor space by placing bunks above play areas. Note vertical rails that prevent the youngsters from falling off the top bunk. The floor is carpeted and provides an instant play surface. (Photo courtesy of Jorges Carpet Mills, Inc.)

One family's approach to decorating a teenage boy's room began with the selection of a wall paneling to serve as a backdrop for posters and other "works of art". The decorative wall is hardboard, which simulates cork. Next came the furniture selection, which includes a corner colonial style dresser and desk with matching free-standing shelf unit. A light contrasting shag carpet offsets the heavy look of the dark furniture. At this point the teenager used his own creativity in hanging model airplanes from the ceiling, displaying miniature motorcycles on the desk and shelves, and adding the many accents that make the room "his". (Photo courtesy of Masonite Corporation)

stressed that the parent keep a color scheme much in mind and maintain a restful environment.

Lofts in a child's room permit some privacy and provide a quiet space for reading or thinking. They also give children a unique opportunity to get a new look at their world, looking down instead of up; the loft lets them see the world from a different angle. It can be considered a very private, special retreat from the family—particularly for teens (see also Chapter 5).

Teens

As the youngster passes into the teens, much can be said for totally turning the room over to him or her for decorating and arranging. The scene may be totally foreign to adult tastes, with posters on every inch of ceiling, items strung from every corner, etc. But the total environment is individualistic and parental approval of it expresses a great deal of love

and acceptance of the child and his ability to make decisions of his own.

ROOM LOCATION

Children's bedrooms may come in all shapes and sizes, but in most instances they are referred to in the housing industry as "secondary" rooms. They are generally smaller than most other rooms in the home. Long rectangular rooms can be made square in appearance through color selection and furniture placement, just as narrow rooms can be made to appear wider via decorating techniques.

Unless you are planning a new home, the location of your child's bedroom has probably already been determined and there is little you can do to change this situation. In planning a new home, however, follow the advice of experts and keep the bedroom

A change in decor using basically the same furnishings enables you to easily update a child's bedroom as he or she grows. The first arrangement at right shows how flexible modulars and homemade plywood cubes fill a young child's storage and play needs. The cubes were "wallcovered" by priming the raw wood, applying wallcovering and then coating with clear polyurethane. Graber's window shades were dressed up with cut-outs of Raggedy Ann and Andy. In reworking the same room (photo above), wallcoverings in a sophisticated pastel reflect a teenager's tastes. The cubes have now been stacked under a board to make a desk and hold plants and a TV. The wall-covered cubes hold snacks for friends, and the dressers line up as a head-board for the bed. Simple plywood cornices cut in points are set over green window shades. (Photos courtesy of Imperial Wallcoverings)

wing separate from the more noisy sections containing kitchen, family room, living room and other gathering areas.

It is also recommended that bedrooms be as convenient as possible to separate or family bathrooms. Many efficient floor plans incorporate a bathroom between two bedrooms, with easy access from both rooms and the hallway (see Chapter 4).

Depending upon the age of the occupant, proximity of the child's bedroom to the parents' master bedroom varies in importance. Most agree that when children are young it is more important that their bedrooms be near that of their parents. As they become teens, it's highly desirable that distance exist between to combat the ever-sounding television, stereo, or other audial background.

WONDER WALLS

Accessories enable the homeowner to radically change the theme of a child's bedroom in no time at all, and with very little cost. Sheets, specifically, need not stay on the bed, for they are stylishly at home on walls, covering a movable screen, a sofa or even a lampshade.

Sheets can satisfy the longing for something new and different each season of the year with major manufacturers offering booklets containing literally hundreds of ideas for room transformations using colorful fabric. Martex™, for example, suggests that entire walls can be quickly covered by putting the sheets up with a staple gun. Or adhesive from the wallpaper store can be used for a more permanent application.

Shirred Sheets

To shirr a wall, measure the width and multiply that by two and one half. Measure the height, add one inch at either end, then add another inch and one half to make a one-inch casing. Stitch the casing, then thread it with string or cable cord. Attach the fabric with staple gun at one end of the wall. Do the same at the other end. Adjust gathers. Then use the staple gun horizontally starting at the top center, then every inch working alternately out to side. Repeat for the bottom.

Hanging Blankets

Dramatic blanket throws are more frequently finding their way off the bed and onto the wall as a focal point. Lions, elephants, horses, panda bears, tigers and other animals are most popular with the young

set. Still other popular children's blanket prints include Star Wars, NFL Playoff, Looney Tunes, Holly Hobbie, and Magic Kingdom.

Alphabet Stencils

For alphabet-age on up, this wall treatment is a sure winner. It takes little more than a base coat of white and pint pots of primary colors. If you don't want to permanently decorate your wall, attach a floor-to-ceiling roll of paper. (See color section for illustration directions.)

Tools and materials 11-inch x 14-inch cardboard for stencils; smaller stencil set to use as a guide; white painted walls; pints of red, yellow and blue paint; extra mixing pails; stiff bristled brushes or foam brushes; masking tape.

Variations Try whatever color scheme you and your child prefer. For example, you might use blue, turquoise, and green as the main colors with accents of yellow. Or for a more grown-up graphic look, stencil in a smashing single color, such as brown.

A compact built-in vanity, with one-piece lavatory-countertop are convenient for a teen's bedroom, and eliminate the need for an expensive additional bathroom. The vanity can be easily installed by tapping into plumbing lines from the bathroom on the other side of the wall that has been paneled with 1'' x 6'' resawn cedar. (Photo courtesy of Western Wood Products Association)

A fabulous tree wood cutout decorates this room. Use the same technique to create your own cutout. (Photo courtesy of American Plywood Association)

Cut-Outs

The real-wood tree shown becomes an unusual decoration for a child's room. If forestry doesn't appeal to your child, use the same technique to create other favorite objects, such as circus clowns, cars, a pretend castle, or animals. Plans are available from the American Plywood Association.

Tools and materials One sheet of ¼-inch APA grade-trademarked plywood; wood stain in brown and green; coping saw; large sheet of brown wrapping paper; sandpaper; adhesive; nails.

Steps

1. Design a free-form tree, following the rough outlines of the tree illustrated. Trunk is one piece; treetop is another. Added contrasting areas in the treetop are separate pieces of plywood.

2. Draw and cut out the tree once you have designed it on kraft paper. Position it on the wall and make whatever adjustments are necessary to have it fill the space.
3. Using your kraft paper pattern, fit the pieces on the plywood sheet and outline them. Cut out pieces.
4. Sand edges and lightly sand front surface.
5. Following stain manufacturer's instructions, experiment with scrap plywood to achieve the depth of stain you need for tree parts. For instance, you may want to use two coats to create a dark green for treetop and edges of "branches" on treetop; and only one coat of lighter green for "branch clusters".
6. Stain actual sections; allow to dry.
7. Attach branch clusters to treetop with panel adhesive or nails. If you use brads or nails, paint heads so they won't show.
8. Attach tree trunk to wall with either nails or adhesive, then attach treetop. (Nailing the tree into a stud will allow easiest removal when you want to change the scheme.)

2
Furniture for Children

A casual tour of any of the famed "merchandise marts" located in major cities for decorator convenience will quickly provide you with a seemingly endless array of furniture for children's rooms. Some of the pieces seem ageless, for they've been around since you were a child, with little revision in design made during the interval. Other items are surprisingly new and interesting, such as the "Cubo," a roll-up foam unit which instantly converts from seating to sleeping purposes. The pillow unit is used partially open for watching TV but opened flat will sleep a six-footer.

The bulk of the specific furniture purchased by the American family for use by children finds its home in the bedroom. And at today's prices, a simple nursery with basic pieces can cost $500; a teen's more formal 7 or 8-piece selection can exceed $1000. However, departures from these ordinary settings can provide the unusual, the more interesting, the more enjoyable, and sometimes the least expensive alternative.

Furniture can strongly influence a child's environment. The California School of Design, San Francisco, best capsulizes the importance of furniture by telling students "we eat, sleep, work, play, love, store, watch, listen, and display all human activity in relation to furniture."

You use furniture all day, every day. You also see it in quantity; while you are using one piece, you are seeing many other pieces. Our concept of the furniture's appearance, combined with its use, constitutes a major factor in choosing those pieces our children may live with for years.

Few of us live the way our parents did, and this change has brought about new furniture that we

Cubo has many moods; use it for playing, relaxing or napping. This polyethylene foam furniture is covered with durable corduroy and is in the design collection of the Museum of Modern Art in New York City. (Photos courtesy of Pasha Pillow Co.)

may not have even recognized as new. For example: the television stand, chairs that fit the body, waterbeds, foam cushions, vinyl upholstery, molded plastics and plywood, and built-in furniture. At the same time, furniture which was popular with our parents is making a resurgence—wicker and rattan, to mention but two items.

Most interior designers trace their livelihood to their ability to search out furniture and accessories that are unusual, and are more interesting than buying a "set" or a "suite." You have this same opportunity in your child's room, and children will often share your enthusiasm for the "find."

CHOOSING FURNITURE

The obvious first consideration in choosing furniture for a child's room is the age. Placing adult-size furniture is almost certain to create frustration. A "chest-on-chest" is great for an adult, but serves little purpose for a child who has to climb on a chair each time to get to the top drawers and their contents. Likewise, few children are comfortable if they have to kneel on a chair to use an adult-height desk 27 to 29 inches off the floor.

Many educators and interior designers believe the best place for the young child is the floor itself. Here

Bunk beds can be purchased with or without a trundle bed to accommodate a third person. This unit, by Bassett, is 70 inches high.

Chest beds offer various storage arrangements for a child's clothing, books and toys. Pictured here are a bed that combines drawers with movable shelves and a bed with three spacious drawers. (Photos courtesy of Bassett Furniture Industries)

a platform unit can be constructed to serve as a bed and storage unit, and can be used for playtime as well. Or a bed may be totally eliminated in favor of a roll-up unit much akin to the familiar sleeping bag. There are few mother-child arguments about making the bed when one need merely roll it up and stick it in the corner. And the floor space gained creates more room for play and games.

Well-planned closets can help replace the need for dresser and chest space. Clear-plastic drawers are now available at many "discount" department stores in a wide range of sizes. These make it easier for the child to find what he's seeking. These drawers can be a lower part of the main clothes closet during the child's younger years, and later rearranged as the child gets older.

Valuable floor space in the bedroom can be saved with Toobline System furniture designed for youngsters. This arrangement places the desk and dresser beneath the upper loft-bed. Other arrangements permit a second bed running either parallel to the loft-bed or at a right angle, still allowing space for a desk below. (Photo courtesy of H.U.D.D.L.E.)

Designed to liberate the imagination and stimulate youthful minds, "Big Toobs" by H.U.D.D.L.E., safeguards little fingers and knees from sharp edges and hard corners.

Types of Construction

In considering the purchase of "customary" children's furniture, you will encounter three basic construction types: solid wood, wood veneer and combination plastic laminate-wood. Each, when well-crafted, is adequate for child use over a long period of time. There is more furniture of lasting quality made today than ever before. While fine handcrafted furniture is still available, machinery has so thoroughly revolutionized woodworking that it is possible not only to duplicate the perfection of the handcraftsman but also improve upon his results.

Attractive solid woods are used for various types of furniture styles—Early American, Italian Renaissance, Jacobean, Gothic, and some modern styles. Furniture frames and the turned, shaped and carved parts of most furniture styles are generally of solid wood construction.

Conversely, the tops, drawers, fronts, doors, and side and end panels on fine furniture are usually veneered or bonded construction. The high-grade cabinet woods are used chiefly as face veneers, and about 90 percent of all wood furniture produced today involves at least some bonded construction.

Plastic laminates in attractive wood grains as well as solid colors are also common today. Intricate drawer and cabinet faces of molded plastic bring the richness of handcrafting within the means of most homeowners. Molded plastic drawers are particularly desirable in children's rooms.

Furniture Pieces — Nursery

In purchasing furniture for a nursery, you'll want to consider the following items:

Crib Usually 53 x 30 inches, 45 to 48 inches high, with both side rails lowerable, plastic free-wheeling casters, adjustable springs and plastic teething rails. U.S. Cribs today must meet Crib Safety Standards as published in the Federal Register November 21, 1973. Many specialists recommend, however, that the child be moved from a crib as soon as he begins to climb. Otherwise the child may fall from as high as four feet, which would be serious. Low box-beds with side rails that keep the child from rolling out are preferable once the child becomes active.

Conventional nursery furniture usually consists of the three pieces shown here: single dresser with foam pad and safety strap, chest and crib. (Photo courtesy of Bassett Furniture Industries)

Dresser Usually with three or more drawers, often with durable plastic laminate top equipped with soft pad and safety strap (for diapering). Height is generally 31 inches while width varies from approximately 42 to 62 inches, with an 18-inch depth.

Chest Approximately 41 to 50 inches high, four or more drawers, approximately 32 to 37 inches wide, and 18 inches deep. Many dressers and chests have a baked-on finish, some have dovetail drawers and center drawer guides for longer wear.

Waterbeds

While most furniture pieces used by children and young adults have been created and designed by adults, there is one notable exception—the waterbed. A student at San Francisco State University, Charles Hall, is widely credited with being the inventor of the first waterbed, a project that grew out of his frustrations to build a truly comfortable chair. To be known as the "Jello Chair", Hall's first invention was a vinyl bag filled with cooking starch and liquid Jello. Though comfortable at first, it quickly became a living blob, cold and clammy, and the user slowly sank to the floor.

But the bed was and is a different matter. In fact, some $235 million worth of waterbeds were sold in 1977, and the market is growing steadily.

At the beginning there was one basic waterbed. Its mattress consisted simply of a vinyl water-filled bag which was then placed on top of an electric heater and fitted into a box-frame base. That model still exists today under the name of the "pure waterbed", with a better grade of vinyl and an improved system for bonding seams.

But there is also the "hybrid waterbed". The difference between most hybrids and the pure waterbed is the lack of the heater in the hybrid. There is, instead, an insulator pad which protects the sleeper from the water's chill, and a foam frame which holds the vinyl water mattress, thus requiring less water and creating a firm edge to the bed.

Technological advances are not the only features offered by the waterbeds. Fashion, more apparent than construction, has been equally as inviting. Many manufacturers are now designing frames to match bedroom sets. Their lines range from the traditional to the contemporary looks.

Inventor Hall says there must be 500 different bed styles on the market today, with the most popular in the $500 price range. He points to statistics which show fifteen percent of Californians sleep on waterbeds and adds that Midwest people still are a bit shy about them.

People with sleep or back problems have found the waterbed most helpful. Hospitals use them to prevent bedsores. Studies at Stanford Medical Center show that premature babies placed in waterbed incubators have a higher survival rate. It is said the warmth and floating sensation nearly approximates the womb environment.

Hammocks

The influence of the sailor's bed is becoming more evident each year, as hammocks find their way into children's rooms. The long-popular "backyard-between-trees bed" provides a guest bed. The unit is a lot more popular with youngsters than is the folding cot or a regular bed.

Many changes have been made in hammock construction since the canvas beds of the great sailing vessels hung from the ship's bulkheads or walls. For one thing, the hammock we know is not used as a winding sheet, as it was in the days of old. If the sailor died at sea, he would be sewn into his hammock and committed to the deep while the captain led the service.

Today's hammock comes in several sizes to accomodate one or more persons. Most units are 11 to 12 feet long so the ends are 6 feet 8 inches (door height) high at the ends and about 2 feet off the floor or ground. The units stretch slightly in use and conform to your body while providing an unbelievably gentle support. The most comfortable resting posi-

The familiar backyard hammock is available in a large selection of sizes and materials. These units are recommended by many designers for children's rooms. (Photo courtesy of House of Hammocks)

tion is diagonal so that your body is nearly level.

The "bed" of the hammock can be of familiar rope construction using flexible cotton or nylon, or it may be most any color in the rainbow, in solids, stripes and patterns. Prices can run anywhere from under $20 to nearly $100, depending upon fabric, construction and size.

Large hammocks (78 x 140 inches or more) are great for playrooms and outdoor play areas, as they can easily handle four small children simultaneously.

FURNITURE YOU BUILD YOURSELF

Numerous items have been used by talented persons to create their own furniture, from simple two-drawer steel file cabinets and flush panel doors to

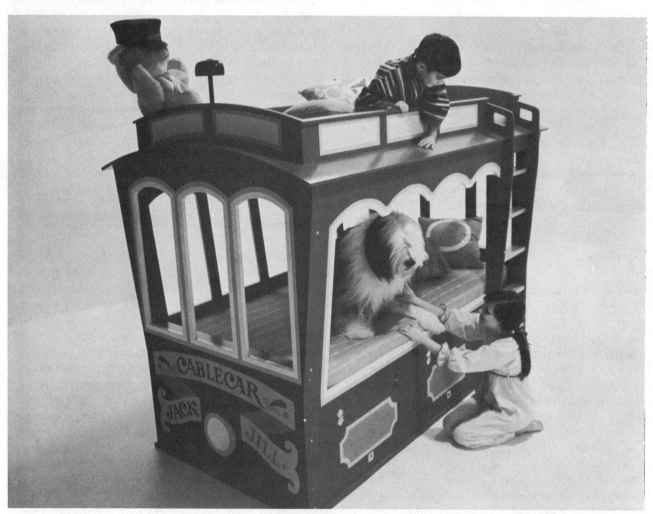

This bed-storage assembly was designed by the American Plywood Association and is constructed with several grades of ¾ and ½-inch plywood. The finished unit can be painted, color-toned or antiqued. The edges can be filled with putty and sanded, or covered with a veneer tape available from building material dealers. (Plans for "Cable Car Bunk Bed" can be obtained from the American Plywood Association.)

create a desk, to large circular "tubes" for "crawl-in" relaxing. Chairs, especially, seem to know no limits. Old tractor seats, nail kegs, suspended netting, canvas slings, and other designs provide a seat in many a child's room.

Create a Super Block for Two

Here is a super system designed by Abbey Darer for GAF Corporation, in which almost all needs, including sleep, storage, study, and game-playing, are incorporated into one unit. The easy-maintenance vinyl flooring by GAF, as well as high-gloss paint and cotton fabric, are all washable. This offers one solution to a tiny room for two tots. The unit provides two beds, a desk/shelf area for two with four drawers each, shelves for games or toys beneath steps and a unique long storage area for skis, etc.

Here is an expanded view of the Superblock. This design for sleeping and activities-for-two uses Gafstar Brite-Bond sheet vinyl in the Bandana pattern. Note that both sleeping areas have guards. Everything is cut from ¾'' plywood and assembled with simple hand tools. Construction breaks down into three major steps (as shown in the drawing below): assembly of the desk unit, attachment of the sides and bed unit, and installaton of the steps and rear wall. Required materials include 12 sheets of 4' x 8' plywood, one flush door, nails, glue and paint. (Photo courtesy of GAF Corporation.)

Tools and materials Twelve sheets of 4 feet x 8 feet x ¾ inch plywood, good one side. One flush door 1½ inches x 18 inches x 6 feet 6 inches or two pieces ¾ inch plywood laminated together (for desk top); eight 1 inch-diameter wood knobs; 2 inch x 1½ inch finishing nails; 1¼-inch round head wood screws; white glue; wood putty; sandpaper; primer-sealer; enamel; circular hand saw; hand tools for assembly.

Flooring is Gafstar Brite-Bond Citation Collection sheet vinyl in "Bandana" pattern. You also need two standard 75 inch x 30 inch cot mattresses, bed linens, etc.

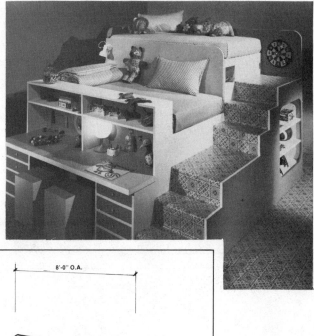

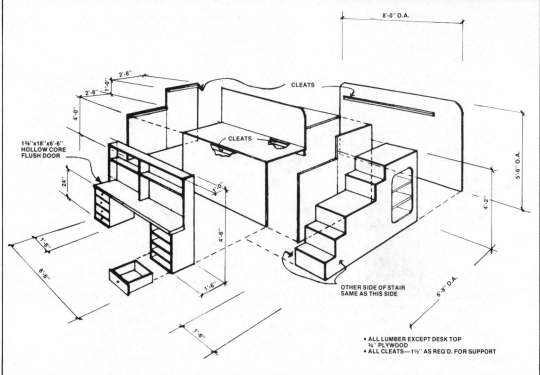

Three Furniture Pieces, One Design

Here is a project that the kids can help with, and they will enjoy the finished project for hours on end. Depending upon which way they stand it, this three-in-one chair can be a rocker, a table, or an everyday chair. Most suitable for younger children, it is one way of providing furniture for modest cost. When youngsters outgrow this furniture, you can consider more permanent furniture to take them through school-age years. The designs are from Georgia-Pacific.

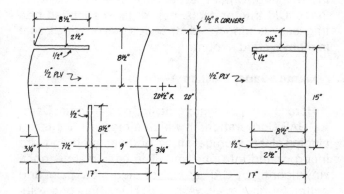

Tools and materials   One ½ inch x 4 foot x 8 foot plywood panel A-B or A-C grade; fine sandpaper; wood filler; sealer; interior semi-gloss enamel paint or stain; 8d finishing nails; drill. (One plywood panel makes two chairs.)

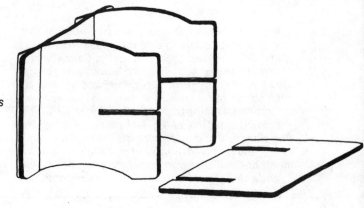

This three-in-one chair can be a rocker, a table or an everyday chair. This easy project is started by measuring and cutting all of the pieces as shown in the diagram. For the curved side panels, cut the pieces square, then use a cardboard or paper pattern for a guide. If you cut the pieces correctly the rocker bottom will balance perfectly. To slot the pieces, pre-drill a hole using a ½'' drill bit at the end of the proposed slot, then cut to the hole. Simply trace the slots of the finished panel onto the un-cut piece to insure a perfect match. Use a wood filler and sealer where necessary, sand and paint. One sheet of plywood is enough to make two chairs. (Project courtesy of Georgia-Pacific)

3
Play Areas—
Indoors & Out

THE PLAYROOM

A playroom, unless properly planned, can create additional work for parents in addition to failing in its intended purpose. All playrooms are subjected to hard use, continual abuse, spills, stains, strewn toys and lots of high-spirited noise.

If the playroom can't take wear and tear, it will age rapidly. But with good planning, a playroom can serve a succession of children for a number of years. And at the end of this period, there will still be the basic walls, floor, ceiling and built-ins that can be redecorated for new functions.

Planning Considerations

To make a playroom as usable as possible, the room needs certain essentials.

Durability Since walls and floors take maximum abuse, they deserve strong defenses. Prefinished hardboard panels which are virtually childproof are a good choice for walls; the panels won't dent, mar or scuff. Stains and soils (including crayon, chalk and fingermarks) wash off easily. A wide variety of finishes—warm wood grains, cheery colors and attractive patterns—are available. For floors, choose a resilient covering—preferably one with a no-wax finish that is easy to clean with soap and water. Or consider the use of washable carpet squares that can be easily replaced if damaged.

Storage Playrooms need plenty. Built-in units with tabletop space and undercounter cabinets work well. Durable plastic laminates in wood tones, bright colors or patterns can add to the decorative theme and at the same time require minimum upkeep. Another practical idea is a storage wall of perforated hardboard paneling. These panels have holes which accept hooks from which a variety of items can be

hung, and brackets on which to mount shelves. Hooks and shelves set low in the wall are easy for small children to reach, so playroom items are more likely to be put away. Also, youngsters like to have their favorite toys on display and readily accessible.

Sound-conditioning This is more easily and economically achieved than most people realize. A number of acoustical ceiling materials are available for sound-control (see Chapter 7). Use of heavy

Tote-boxes long have been used by adults for numerous tasks about the home. This one's designed specifically for the child, made of plywood and painted a bright red. It has two convenient compartments, one with door and the other with window. (Photo courtesy of American Plywood Assn.)

drapery and carpeting or cushioned flooring helps deaden noise transmission to the rest of the house. What you put on the walls also makes a difference. Even hardboard paneling installed over commonly used backup materials makes a good sound insulator.

It is most important that the furniture used in the playroom is scaled to the size of the youngster. Small table-and-chair sets will prompt more enjoyable play time than the standard, higher table and chairs used by adults.

Playroom Suggestions

Children especially like modular boxes which can be arranged and rearranged at will. These units can be easily constructed from plywood, painted bright colors and serve many functions. Such boxes can be seats, tables, "blocks", storage cubicles and other "imaginary" items.

Sprawling train and car race track set-ups can be made more usable and enjoyable by securing the track to a sheet of plywood hinged at the base of a wall. When not in use, the panel can be raised via pulleys until it is parallel with the wall and out of the traffic pattern.

Here are some other playroom ideas that have proven successful:

- Use chalkboard-finish hardboard for the table top and mount it on legs at a height where children can sit on it and draw.

- Include sections of tackboard on the walls of the room so youngsters can create their own decor with finished crayoning, paste-ups, etc.

- Use open-front bookcases for doll houses, each shelf being a different "room" or "floor" in the home.

- Build storage chests to foam-mattress size to provide a nap-time corner.

- Equip undercounter storage sections with casters so the child can move the entire contents to another place in the room.

- If a television set is to be included in the room, place it on a swivel table so it can be directed at various play areas within the room.

- Where possible, include a small sink with drinking fountain attachment.

Circus-time toys are playroom favorites and provide movable storage to encourage the youngster to pick up at the end of playtime. (Photo courtesy of American Plywood Assn.)

BUILDING HINTS:

1. Trace cutting and painting patterns onto plywood. Some patterns are complete. Others, like the pieces R on the Circus Wagon, must be flopped over to trace the second half of the pattern. The cutting pattern for the Circus Wagon is represented by a solid red line. (The thinner red lines identify the areas to be painted.) The cutting patterns and paint diagrams can be traced on the plywood. Then turn the paper pattern over and repeat the process to obtain the full pattern for each piece.

2. Cut out the plywood pieces and assemble the box, gluing and nailing as required. Ornamentation will be added later.

3. Drill a 1-1/2 in. hole in each H piece as shown. Glue-nail the four H pieces to the bottom of the wagon. Glue and screw the wheels and hubcaps together. Glue six evenly spaced spokes to each wheel. Insert the 1-1/2 in. axle dowels through the holes and attach wheel apparatus (including spacers) as shown.

4. Drill a 1-1/4 in. hole in each K piece for the dowel. Glue and screw the K pieces to the front of the cart. Insert the dowel. Glue and screw the top and bottom handle I pieces to the dowel.

5. Glue ornamentation in appropriate places as shown.

6. Fill any gaps in exposed plywood edges with wood dough. Sand smooth when dry.

7. Finish with latex paint. Suggested colors are identified within the cutting pattern.

MATERIALS LIST:

Recommended plywood:	A-B Interior, A-C Exterior, or Medium Density Overlaid (MDO) APA® grade-trademarked plywood.

PLYWOOD

Quantity	Description
1 panel	1/2 in. x 4 ft x 8 ft plywood

OTHER MATERIALS:

Quantity	Description
37 ft	1/2 in. half-rounds cut to various lengths for ornamentation
4-1/2 ft	1/2 in. half-rounds for spokes (cut in 2-1/4 in. lengths)
43 in.	1-1/2 in. dowel for axles (cut in two 21-1/2 in. pieces)
10 in.	1-1/4 in. dowel for attaching handle to wagon
As required	#6 wood screws
As required	6d finishing nails
As required	White or urea-resin glue, wood dough, fine sandpaper, top quality latex paint

CIRCUS WAGON TOY BOX

exploded view

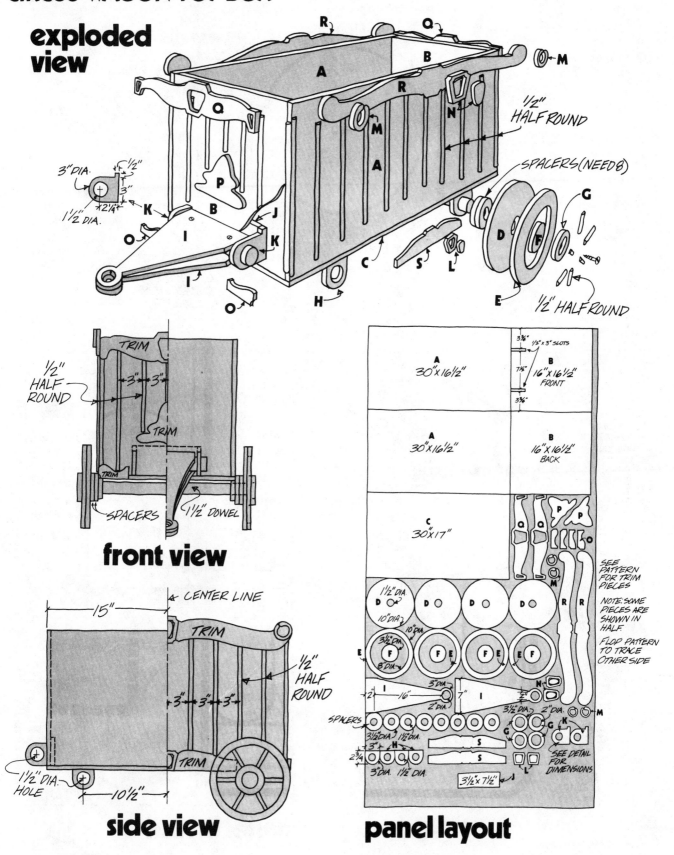

3" DIA.
1/2"
3"
x 2 1/4"
1 1/2" DIA.

1/2" HALF ROUND

SPACERS (NEED 8)

1/2" HALFROUND

front view

TRIM

1/2" HALF ROUND

TRIM

TRIM

SPACERS

1 1/2" DOWEL

side view

CENTER LINE

15"

TRIM

1/2" HALF ROUND

3" 3" 3"

TRIM

1 1/2" DIA. HOLE

10 1/2"

panel layout

A 30"x16 1/2"

B 16"x16 1/2" FRONT
3/16"
1/2"x 3" SLOTS
7/8"
3/16"

A 30"x16 1/2"

B 16"x16 1/2" BACK

C 30"x17"

SEE PATTERN FOR TRIM PIECES

NOTE: SOME PIECES ARE SHOWN IN HALF.

FLOP PATTERN TO TRACE OTHER SIDE

1 1/2" DIA.
10" DIA.

3 1/2" DIA.
8" DIA.

2" 16" 7"
3" DIA.
2" DIA.

SPACERS
3 1/2"DIA. 1 1/2"DIA.
3" H
2 3/4"
3" DIA. 1 1/2" DIA.

3 1/2"x 7 1/2"

SEE DETAIL FOR DIMENSIONS

SEAL DESK AND CHAIR

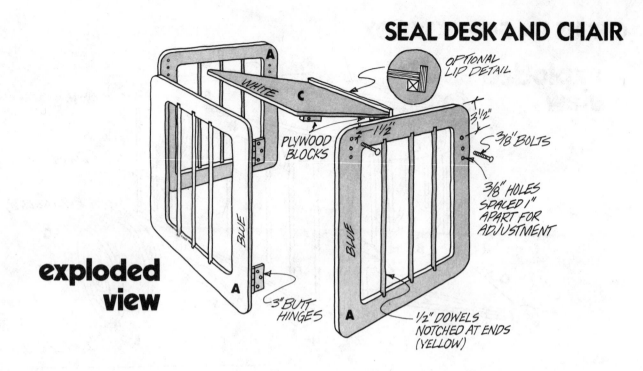

OPTIONAL LIP DETAIL

WHITE

C

PLYWOOD BLOCKS

1½"

3½"

3/8" BOLTS

3/8" HOLES SPACED 1" APART FOR ADJUSTMENT

BLUE

BLUE

A

A

3" BUTT HINGES

½" DOWELS NOTCHED AT ENDS (YELLOW)

exploded view

SEAT BOTTOM

LOOP

½" DOWEL

CUSHION IS FITTED WITH LOOP

seat details

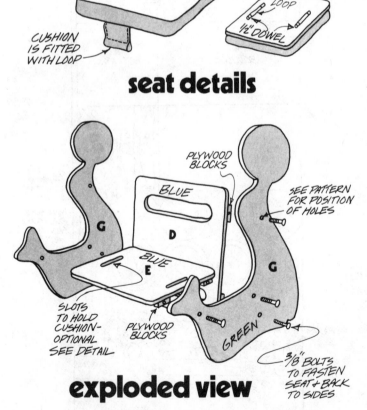

PLYWOOD BLOCKS

BLUE

D

SEE PATTERN FOR POSITION OF HOLES

G

BLUE

E

G

SLOTS TO HOLD CUSHION- OPTIONAL SEE DETAIL

PLYWOOD BLOCKS

GREEN

3/8" BOLTS TO FASTEN SEAT & BACK TO SIDES

exploded view

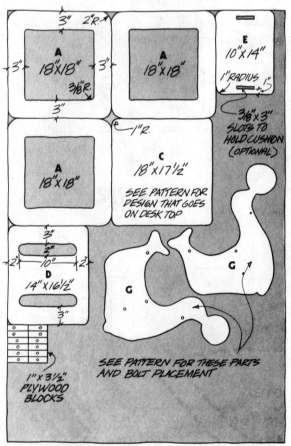

3" 2"R.

3"

A 18"X18"

3"

A 18"X18"

E 10"X14"

1" RADIUS

1"

3/8" X 3" SLOTS TO HOLD CUSHION (OPTIONAL)

3/8"R.

1"R.

A 18"X18"

C 18"X17½"

SEE PATTERN FOR DESIGN THAT GOES ON DESK TOP

3"

2"

2" 10" 2"

D 14"X16½"

3"

G

G

G

1" X 3½" PLYWOOD BLOCKS

SEE PATTERN FOR THESE PARTS AND BOLT PLACEMENT

panel layout

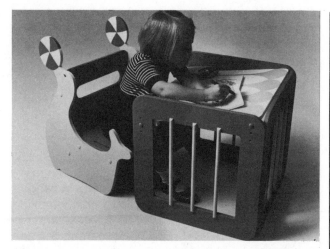

Easy-to-make furniture such as this all-plywood desk-seat arrangement prompts playtime activity far more than having the youngster sit at the kitchen table. (Photo courtesy of American Plywood Assn.)

BUILDING HINTS:

1. Trace the cutting and painting patterns onto the plywood. The cutting pattern for the Seal Chair and Cage Desk is represented by the gray area. (NOTE: The desk top pattern is for painting purposes only. It is NOT a cutting pattern.)

2. Carefully cut out the plywood pieces.

3. Desk assembly: First cut four 1 in. x 3-1/2 in. blocks from the scrap plywood. Glue-nail blocks and optional lip detail to desk top as indicated. Notch the 1/2 in. dowels on both ends as shown, and glue-nail in place on desk front and sides. Attach butt hinges to desk front and sides. Align desk top and sides. Then drill carriage bolt holes through desk sides into desk top blocks as shown. After the four main carriage bolt holes are drilled, drill two additional holes below each top hole on desk sides. Bolt desk sides and top together, using the appropriate side hole to adjust the desk to your child's height.

4. Chair assembly: First cut oblong holes in chair back and seat pieces as shown. Then cut four 1 in. x 3-1/2 in. seat supports and four 1 in. x 3-1/2 in. back supports from scrap plywood. Glue-nail seat and back supports in positions indicated. Align seal chair sides with chair back. Then drill carriage bolt holes through seal sides into back support blocks. Insert carriage bolts. Align seat with seal sides, and drill through seal sides into seat supports. Assemble chair by fastening remaining carriage bolts in place.

5. Fill any plywood edge gaps with wood dough. Sand smooth when dry.

6. Finish with top quality latex paint. Suggested colors are identified on cutting pattern. When paint is dry, install seat cushion if desired.

MATERIALS LIST:

Recommended plywood: A-B Interior, A-C Exterior, or Medium Density Overlaid (MDO) APA® grade-trademarked plywood

PLYWOOD:

Quantity	Description
1 panel	1/2 in. x 4 ft x 8 ft plywood

OTHER MATERIALS:

Quantity	Description
12	2 in. x 3/8 in. carriage bolts
11 ft	1/2 in. dowel cut in nine 13-1/2 in. lengths (remaining dowel can be cut in two 3 in. pieces for chair cushion)
4	3 in. butt hinges
As required	6d finishing nails
As required	Wood dough, fine sandpaper, white or urea-resin glue, top quality latex paint

A fun carpet quickly established the setting for this family playroom where countless games can be enjoyed while relaxing on the floor. Among the games are chess, checkers, hop-scotch, Parchesi, tic-tac-toe and spin-out. The colorful carpeting is made of Antron II to resist wear and soil and comes complete with component game kits. (Photo courtesy of Jorges Carpet Mills, Inc.)

PLAY YARDS

Exact theories on home play yards for children are perhaps as numerous as the parents who plan them —and, also as diverse. Get a group of parents together for a discussion on "what we should put in the back yard for Dick and Jane" and you'll soon have a heated discussion on your hands.

Many parents are of the opinion that children should be almost totally unstructured in their outdoor play. On the other side is the argument that planned play spaces help to direct the child in learning, and keep the child from being bored.

The author takes the middle ground (where it is much safer) and believes that some of both are good and should be incorporated into any area of the yard set aside for children's use. Age of the children, of course, further dictates what should be done, as does geographic location.

If one is to believe in childhood and its many exciting discoveries, he must at the same time believe that water, sand, trees, grass, plants, animals and other natural elements contribute to enjoyable play time. Think but for a moment of the hours spent as a youth with nothing more available than packable snow which was converted to a snowman (before the snowperson arrived), forts, hideaways, castles and other childhood "spaces".

Sand Box Variations

Little has to be done to improve the imagination of a young child when he or she is given a sand box, sand and some water to make creation possible. Sand boxes needn't be more than four 2 x 12's forming a box on bare earth, although more elegant models may include a lift-off top that makes the box a garden seat when the children are not at play.

This same structure can be lined with poly-ethylene sheeting to become a water pond for the myriad of uses a young mind will conjure. Duct tape available at building material dealers will permit joining the sheets together; the sheets are easy to drain, fold and store away when interest runs thin.

Trends

A trip to nearly any new neighborhood park will give you the direction play yards have taken in recent years. In place of the old swings with dangerous solid wood or metal seats, you'll find nonmoving designs that encourage the child to move and explore. Sawed-off telegraph poles placed at varying heights encourage climbing and balancing. All forms of climbing and hanging bars develop and strengthen young muscles. Barrels and pipe provide tunnels to climb through. Earth is for molding; mazes are for exploring.

Redwood boards and tree rounds were used to create this interesting children's play structure placing emphasis on climbing and balancing. A tan bark ground cover minimizes maintenance and eliminates tracking mud into the home on wet days. (Photo courtesy of California Redwood Assn.)

BUILD A SANDBOX

Outdoor wood which as been pressure treated with preservative chemicals to resist decay and insects was used in the construction of this backyard sandbox. The wood retains its natural appearance with painting and is clean-to-the-touch. Only eight boards were required to complete the 5-foot-square unit which has six inches of sand atop a two-inch gravel base. Galvanized nails were used to prevent rust stains. (Photo courtesy of Koppers Co.)

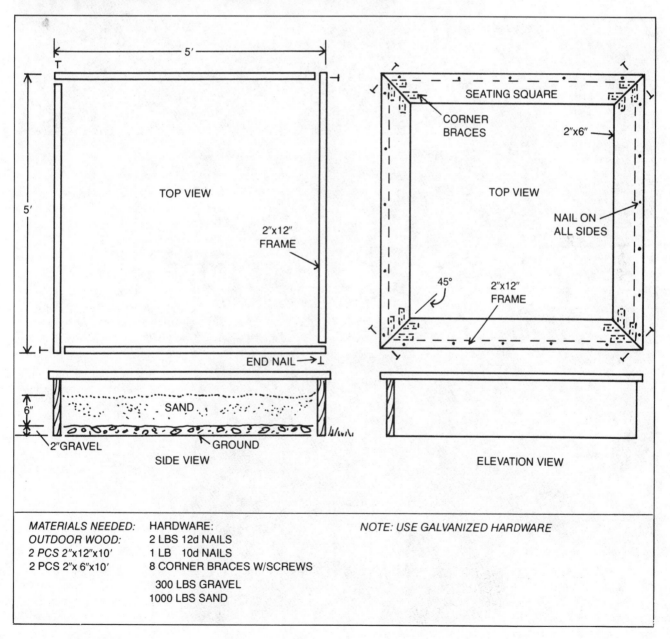

MATERIALS NEEDED:	HARDWARE:	NOTE: USE GALVANIZED HARDWARE
OUTDOOR WOOD:	2 LBS 12d NAILS	
2 PCS 2"x12"x10'	1 LB 10d NAILS	
2 PCS 2"x 6"x10'	8 CORNER BRACES W/SCREWS	
	300 LBS GRAVEL	
	1000 LBS SAND	

Hillside homes can include safe play areas even for little tots like those enjoying this floor-level deck of post-and-beam construction. Note the horizontal-style railing which keeps youngsters from climbing through or getting their head stuck. (Photo courtesy of Western Wood Products Assn.)

The exterior design of the home often opens the door to unusual play yard possibilities. This arrangement utilizes redwood lumber and a few stepped-up tree rounds to meet the climbing urge of each youngster. The ladder type hanging rail is suspended from the deck by metal brackets. (Photo courtesy of California Redwood Assn.)

Designer Roger Fleck looks upon this structure as more than a fortress, a mountain, castle, tower, cave, dungeon and tunnel—he believes it's all these things to children and doubles as a storage facility for trikes, wagons and the like. It's a completely prefabricated unit made of redwood and fir plywood, with brightly colored doors hinged down on all four sides so that kids' things and kids can enter and exit safely and easily. The unit is 8'6" x 8'6" x 8' high and has an interior volume of approximately 250 cu. ft. (Photo courtesy of California Redwood Assn.)

The elimination of turn-taking equipment puts all children on an equal basis and opens the door to total-time enjoyment. Less space is required for more children, and the educational aspect increases far more rapidly.

All of this is not to eliminate the fun of swinging, sliding down a board and revolving on a merry-go-round, all items of which are most "at home" in many residential play yards. The old tire swing still hangs from many a tree across the country, as hopefully it will for generations to come.

In planning your play yard, give special consideration to setting it apart from the rest of the landscape so the children can experience pride of ownership. A fence, well planned hedges, or other barriers, can help define the area and at the same time hide the clutter that's sure to occur. Try to plan the area in a grassy space out of the routine traffic pattern from the house or patio and beyond the other play areas.

Sand, tan bark and tree mulch are excellent ground covers that help to keep down mud, as does initial good drainage. Header boards will assist in keeping cover in its rightful place.

Play sculpture in the residential play yard can be as stimulating to the adult who creates it as the youngster who uses it. Wood, steel, concrete, rope and many discarded industrial elements can be put to use including large wire spools, discarded doors, crates and boxes, barrels, ladders, steel drums, tires, etc. Items that can be taken apart and reassembled by children in still different forms are most exciting.

Playhouses

Playhouses and treehouses greatly expand any home play yard and initiate countless hours of fantasy time for the youngsters. Such structures may require a building permit from your local city hall while still other areas may prohibit them altogether. Be sure to check before adding either; many a disappointed youngster has watched as a non-code-conforming structure has been removed. Also, keep in mind future use of the structure—especially the grade-level playhouse—for storage, or an adult relaxation area once the children have forgotten its existence. (See *Successful Playhouses* by John Boeschen)

Game Areas

Game areas can begin with just a tetherball roped to a common plumbing pipe set in a tire-concrete base. This assembly is easy to make, heavy enough to remain upright, and can be rolled from one location to another as desired. Shuffle boards of poured concrete or asphalt also are popular with pre-teens and teens. When painting such courts outdoors, buy traffic paint from your dealer for longer-lasting results.

Play areas can be created along property lines in many areas where high fences are permitted by the city building department. Here the play platform and walkway were constructed of 2x4-inch douglas fir while wood chips were used as the ground cover to keep down weeds, dust and eliminate tracking mud into the house. The low fence in the foreground is a pleasant background for landscaping as well as a partial screen between the play area and lawn area of the yard. (Photo courtesy of Western Wood Products Assn.)

4
The Bathroom

When it comes to designing and decorating a bathroom for primarily children's use, the overriding factor should be practicality. This room too often is initially planned for adults with little thought, if any, given to its use by youngsters who will be splashing at walls and floors on a daily basis.

Considerable change has been made in the American bathroom, but the least of this change has been directed toward youngsters. Visit any new home development and you'll find master baths flaunting an elegance that sells the house. Such baths are important, but so are those that will be used by children.

While every home most certainly cannot be equipped with a separate bathroom for each bedroom, it is highly desirable that a specific bathroom be set aside for children. If the home is small and one bathroom must meet the needs of all, it should be large enough and planned to accommodate more than one person at a time. Such baths can be compartmentalized for desired privacy. A partition which separates the lavatories from the tub/toilet area adds privacy and convenience. Some bathrooms go one step further, with separate private "zones" for each fixture and a common "dressing room". This design works extremely well for a large family.

FIXTURES

Tubs

The bathtub today comes in many styles and sizes, including space-saving corner models, square shapes with circular tub area, deep tubs for steeping comfort, safe tubs with slip-resistant bottoms and safety grip handles, tubs with body contour designs for stretch-out soaking, tubs with whirlpool for hydro-massage, and numerous combination tub-shower arrangements.

Cast iron and formed steel still are the most used materials for bathtub construction, but heavy-duty fiberglass-reinforced polyester is making dramatic inroads because of one-piece construction and crisp lines not possible with older materials. The plastic units are easy to maintain with liquid cleaner and are ideal for remodeling purposes because of their lighter weight.

Lavatories

No other bathroom fixtures come in as many styles, sizes and shapes as the lavatory. Because it is often surrounded by attractive light fixtures, medicine cabinet, countertop, vanity, etc., the area it occupies becomes the focal point in the average bathroom.

With such a variety of choices available, it is possible to select lavatories that fit the needs of children as well as adults. Realizing that the lavatory may be needed for washing delicate garments, in addition

Kohler's multi-purpose lavatory for bedroom or bathroom is designed to expand as the child grows. Initially it can be used for a miniature bath, later for teenage shampoo lavatory. The drop-in fixture measures 28x19 in. and has a roomy 23x14 in. sloping basin.

The circus theme employed here helps encourage a child's acceptance of "tub time", while the fixtures are designed for both personal and room cleanliness. Among the desirable features for a child's bath are: splashproof tub enclosure with wall safety bar, bathtub with safety grab rails, vinyl flooring, plastic laminate countertop with removable safety bar for baby diapering, off-the-floor water closet, bidet, shampoo lavatory and reachable child storage. (Photo courtesy of Kohler Co.)

to washing face and hands and shampooing, a small lavatory should be used only when lack of space is an overriding problem.

The most popular lavatory for new construction and remodeling is the self-rimming model that seals directly to countertops for neater, quicker installation and minimum maintenance. Still other models install directly on vanity cabinets with metal ring or frame holding the unit in place, under tile, marble or plastic laminate countertops.

Fixture installation standards for lavatories call for a minimum depth of 16 inches for the countertop extension from the wall surface, with the average counter in the 20-to-24-inch range. Twin lavatories

should be installed with a minimum 16 inches from the center of one bowl to the center of the other bowl. Greater spacing is highly desirable when children are to use the fixtures.

Most lavatories used by adults are installed 34 to 38 inches from floor to top of the bowl. This dimension frequently is reduced to 31 inches when children 5 feet 2 inches or shorter are to use the fixture. Keep in mind that the initial height selected can be modified at a later date by adding a new cabinet and longer supply and drain lines. Mirrors and medicine cabinets should be a minimum of 8 inches above the countertop-bowl surface to minimize splashing problems.

Space limitations frequently associated with creating a new children's bathroom can be partially solved by using a corner tub installation. This Mayflower model by Kohler has an integral corner seat which can also serve as a handy shelf for soaps and toiletries. The bath measures 48x44x50 in. from corner to front, and is 14 in. high.

Toilets

In selecting a toilet, keep in mind that all toilets are not alike. Some look better, some work better, and others offer more convenience features than others. Some save water; some offer off-the-floor mounting for easier cleaning, and others have low silhouettes and space-saving designs.

The toilet is semi-automatic in its function and requires the proper relation between water volume and interior design to create an efficient waste disposal system. Most home units consist of a bowl and a tank which stores sufficient water for a proper flushing action.

Most toilets are available with either round or elongated bowl rims. The elongated bowl (sometimes referred to as "extended rim") is 2 inches longer from the front edge of the rim to the back of the toilet. This shape is recommended for children as being more sanitary and easier to keep clean.

Off-the-floor toilets require 2 x 6 support studding instead of the conventional 2 x 4 studs used in most home walls. This can be accomplished quite simply during new construction or for add-on rooms; however, it is more difficult to install in an existing wall.

Toilets should be installed with one inch clearance from the back wall, a minimum 18 inches from a facing wall or cabinet, and minimum 15 inches

from the center of the bowl to each side wall or cabinet. Keep in mind that replacing an outdated toilet is not a major undertaking. The existing plumbing will accommodate newer fixtures, and new water supply lines are relatively inexpensive.

Fittings

Plumbing fittings for a child's bathroom should be of the premixed type whenever possible. Handle and dial models that control both hot and cold water with a single hand are far easier for the young child to handle than are two-valve units with two handles. The single-control fitting enables control of water temperature by movement of the control to the right or left. The volume is controlled by moving the same control in and out, or backward and forward.

Two other "wise investments" in selecting bathroom fittings for children's use are "pressure balancing" and "thermostatic" controls. Volume on the pressure balancing valve is usually preset and the valve maintains that temperature automatically, preventing scalds. This is accomplished by a pressure-sensing device that automatically decreases the flow of either the hot or the cold water when the operating pressure in the opposite line drops. Should the pressure of the cold water supply drop sufficiently to cause scalding, the valve automatically shuts off the hot water flow. This pressure balancing valve is most commonly found controlling a showerhead.

The thermostatic control employs a heat-sensing device to automatically adjust the hot and cold volume to maintain a preselected temperature of mixed water. This type of valve gives a more precise temperature than the pressure balancing valve, and it usually permits the user to control volume as well as temperature.

Shower Fittings

Another bathroom fitting that is growing rapidly in popularity, particularly for use by children, is the personal shower that offers the bather the convenience of leaving the shower head in place in a wall-mount, or detaching a flexible hose to hold the unit in hand. Most of the major firms that manufacture

Most home showers with their too-high-for-children shower heads can be easily adapted to child use with the installation of a hand-held shower. This 3-spray unit by Ondine quickly attaches to a wall shower arm or special tub spout to provide three different water flows—massage spray, soft aerated spray or regular spray. Flexible hose length for most models is 59 inches and other lengths are available on request. This type unit has a wall mount that can be positioned at any height.

◄*Plastic laminates are an excellent material to use in the children's bath. If they get splashed they can be quickly wiped clean and new. This room was designed as a combination mudroom-bath with twin lavatories and a low-level mirror for child use. The brick floor takes hard usage, although the irregular surface complicates cleaning. (Photo courtesy of Formica Corp.)*

personal showers offer products that give the bather a choice of two or three different sprays in the same head—sprays to massage, knead, pound, stroke, pulsate, tingle, or bubble.

Although personal showers are designed to replace a regular shower head, some manufacturers make a diverter valve to allow the choice of using the hand shower or the regular head. Diverter heads can also be used to outfit bathtub spouts with a hand shower operation.

Mounting accessories for personal showers include chrome-plated wall bars in 24 or 42 inch lengths to permit sliding the shower head up and down so that it can be positioned high for adults and low for small children. Hose length for most models is approximately 5 feet, but shorter and longer hoses are readily available.

American-Standard designers planned this bathroom for easy alteration to a guest bath once it served its original childhood years' needs. The 39x38 in. space-saving tub leaves room for a low-seat toy box while inexpensive ladders keep towels at child-reach height. The dressing table lavatory permits use of a chair.

LIGHTING

Proper lighting in the bathroom is just as important for children as for adults. There should be good overall plus specialized lighting in key areas. Balanced lighting on either side of the mirrors is ideal for teens as they enter the make-up/shaving phase of life.

There should be a light over the tub and in the shower and most designers will strongly recommend the use of a combination light-ventilating fan in the shower to remove the steam before it fogs mirrors. Improvements in fluorescent lighting lamps make them highly usable in the bathroom, and on a par with incandescents long known for providing "true" color for make-up.

Space permitting, medicine cabinets should not be placed directly over the lavatory. Side wall or corner installations provide better utility and allow large, well-illuminated mirror expanse. (For additional details on lighting for the bathroom, see Chapter 7.)

STORAGE

It's one thing to accessorize the children's bath, and another to clutter. Cosmetics and such sundries should be concealed in nearby storage areas, drawers and the like. Handy-height wood or chrome ladders are excellent for youngster towel storage. Face towels require an 18-inch bar per pair, with a hanging depth of 15 to 23 inches. Bath towels require a 24-inch per pair bar width with a hanging depth of 20 to 24 inches. A commonly used rule-of-thumb calls for 27 inches of rod space per person. Towel bars in most bathrooms are installed 36 to 42 inches off the floor.

WALLCOVERINGS

Vinyls

Vinyls are a good choice for the bathroom because they are washable, strippable, and have a relatively high resistance to the moisture that results from showers and baths. Because changes in heat and humidity can loosen wallcovering, it is important to hang the material properly. For paper-backed vinyl wallcovering, use a vinyl adhesive. For cloth-backed, use a mixture of part powdered vinyl plus part premixed. This use of a vinyl adhesive rather than a wheat paste will prevent mildew. (See Chapter 8 for instructions on hanging wallpaper.)

Ceramic Tiles

Ceramic tile is probably the most popular material used for floors and walls in the bathroom. In addition to the traditional singly-applied tiles, there are now available "sheet squares" of tile applied to a backing that can be put up in blocks, with grout added between tiles afterward.

Space permitting, the family bath can serve adults on one side and children on the other as shown here. Folding doors are used to save valuable wall space, and the built-in lavatory-vanity unit on the children's side has a pull out "step-drawer" for the little ones. (Photo courtesy of Armstrong Cork Co.)

Wasted attic space was remodeled into a teenager's retreat with fold-down hanging desk, wall-hung shelving, cabinets built under the sofabed and efficient lighting. The room is fully carpeted and has easy-to-maintain walls of 1x8-inch V-groove western wood paneling. Note below the desk that other storage has been fitted into the lower part of the sloping walls. (Photo courtesy of Western Wood Products Assn.)

5
Retreats:
Attics, Studies,
Basements

Parents are quick to recognize that preteens and teenagers often cannot be lumped together with younger children. They are a separate kind of human being—neither child nor adult—and industries of every description are vying to supply their special needs as well as the special psychological approach they seem to require of parents these days. It's no secret then that the parent is being pushed to offer separate-but-equal quarters to preteens and adolescents, for the sakes of all parties. Accordingly, this chapter presents alternatives that will satisfy the need for privacy and individualism, and peace and quiet. Retreats in the attic and basement are covered, as well as study areas set apart as much as possible from everyday traffic.

ATTICS

Skylights

The recent dramatic improvements in skylights have greatly expanded the possibilities of converting wasted attic space into additional living space. Where it was once necessary to build an expensive dormer into the roof to provide required natural light and ventilation, you now can cut a hole in the roof and install a weatherproof, operable window.

Skylights today come in all shapes and sizes with clear or translucent glass or plastic, with most units offered in "package" form for homeowner installation. Most are double glazed to provide necessary insulation and some are tinted to filter the sun and eliminate glare.

Manufacturers produce skylights to fit snugly between standard rafter spacing on 16, 32, and 48-inch centers. The needed opening is cut from inside the attic, and roofing materials are then removed and replaced according to the specific instructions provided with each particular style and brand skylight.

Direction of the natural light can be straight, angled or flared depending upon unit selection.

Conversion Considerations

In most homes, the attic generally serves as a "catch-all" for items placed there for future use.

Opening up a section of the roof and closing it in again with windows or skylights helps to make attic space usable for children's rooms. The wallcovering and matching window shades depict memorabilia hailing back to the days of the clipper ships. (Photo courtesy of Wallcovering Industry Bureau.)

Simple frame for canopy bed helps turn an attic space into a girl's retreat. (Photo courtesy of GAF Corp.)

Many attics have full or partial subfloors; most are unheated; all should be insulated regardless of their use to both save energy and make the balance of the home more comfortable for daily living.

More than any other room in the home, the attic best accommodates built-in furniture that conserves space and makes best use of low, sloping roof lines and short "knee" walls. Built-in beds, for example, can be placed along the short walls while the higher-ceiling center area of the room is better used for person movement. Likewise, extended dormer areas already in existence in many homes provide an excellent location for study desks built between flanking walls.*

Many attic knee walls also hold the key to added organized storage gained through the simple installation of a pywood floor and access doors leading from the reclaimed room area.

Decor Tip: Cover All Mix-Matched Surfaces Scrubbable fabric-backed vinyl wallcovering is strong enough to be used on many interesting surfaces. To coordinate a room that is cut up spatially—such as converted attic space—use the same covering throughout. Apply it to walls, built-in fronts, and even free-standing pieces such as tables or sides of cubed furniture.

STUDY AREAS

The home study center, when well planned and well lighted, is a considerable asset that can be expected to pay lifetime dividends. Many youngsters find themselves faced with up to five hours of school homework or study each day, with only an inadequate study location such as the kitchen table, card table or dining table.

Eye Needs

General Electric's lighting experts at famed Nela Park have spent years of research on the proper home study center and report that home study involves the elements of concentration, a fixed position, and critical eye use—elements which must be properly correlated for the student if his studying is to be effective. The ease, comfort, efficiency and accuracy with which the student's eyes perform

*For additional desk and file projects, with specific instructions, see "Home Offices" in **Successful Shelves & Built-Ins** by Jay Hedden.*

are dependent upon the quality and quantity of lighting in his visual field and on the study task.(See also Chapter 7.)

In planning a home study center, parents should strive to provide an area in which the student is relaxed and comfortable. Of major importance is a permanent, level work surface that is the student's own, always ready and equipped for his study needs. A flat-top desk or table, with a top surface of about 24 x 46 inches, gives sufficient working space. The surface should be nonreflective, and light in color. If the surface is dark it should be covered with a pastel blotter or construction paper.

The desk should be positioned flat against a wall (never in front of a window) and away from family activity or conversation areas. If the wall is dark or boldly patterned, cover the area in front of the desk with light-colored tackboard or pegboard.

In supplying children storage areas in the home, often times a special-purpose area can be part of the scheme. Here an ell-shaped loft was transformed into a library-study hall-game center. The built-in bookcases have adjustable shelves and a series of "map" drawers for art prints and the like. Walls of the stairwell are paneled with clear finished hemlock for easy upkeep. (Photo courtesy of Western Wood Products Assn.)

The desk surface should be 28 to 29 inches above the floor to accommodate an adjustable-posture chair seat that will raise the student and correctly locate his eye level in relation to the desk top. General Electric engineers recommend the eye position should be at least 14 inches above the work surface. Books and other reading matter should be propped or tilted about 30 degrees toward the eyes. If the book is flat on the work surface, the type is shortened and reading is more difficult.

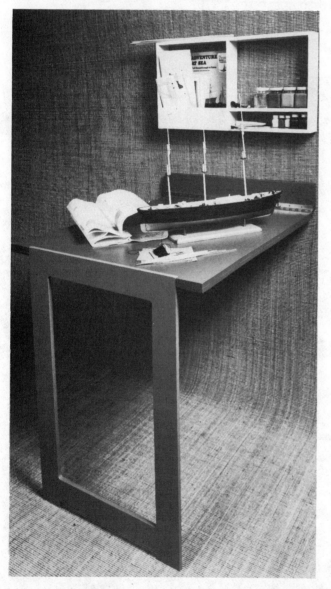

Bare minimum in a home study center is this fold-down work table which can be stored against the wall when not in use. The support frame is piano-hinged, as is the other end of the desk. (Photo courtesy of American Plywood Association.)

A pair of lamps, either wall-hung or table-based, provide the best work lighting, since light comes from two directions to cover the whole desk top. However, most homes do not have a study desk large enough to accommodate a pair of table-based lamps. Also, decorative appropriateness for the desk and for the room must be considered in deciding between a single lamp or a pair, or between wall-hung versus table-type lamps.

Because it is so close to the eye, a lamp shade that is dark in color or that transmits too great an amount of light can be a source of distraction, annoyance, and eye strain. The inside should be white, or nearly so, to reflect the light efficiently over the work area. An example of an inefficient study lamp is the popular two-globe Colonial lamp; it makes an attractive decoration, but puts too high a brightness right in the user's eyes.

Table-based lamps should measure 15 to 16 inches from table top to bottom edge of the shade. This assures the user's eyes will be nearly in line with the lower edge of the shade when he is in normal reading position.

Because study lamps are nearly always located close to and in front of the student's work and the student's eyes, it is important that these lamps be equipped with diffusing bowls or discs to soften reflected glare. The shade should flare at the bottom for best distribution of light. Minimum diameters for shade bottoms are 16 inches for a single table-based lamp, 15 inches for a single wall-hung lamp, and 10 inches for a wall-hung lamp when used in a pair.

Placement of the desk table lamp (or window) is best at the left side of a right-handed person. Wall-mounted scissor-bracket lamps are recommended for desks deeper than 24 inches, as these fixtures can be pulled out nearer the front edge of the desk when in use and pushed back against the wall when not in use.

While tens of thousands of "bullet" lamps have been sold for desk use, these fixtures have a major drawback in that they put a hot spot on the book being read, washing out the contrast of black print on white page, and reducing visibility. This type of lamp, no matter how well placed, cannot provide full, even illumination on the study area.

Fluorescent lamps teamed with incandescent lamps can provide excellent light for a student study center. Lighting specialists suggest the fluorescent light source be no more than 12 inches back from the front edge of the desk or table to prevent reflection in the user's eyes (see sketch). A 30-watt 36 inch deluxe warm white tube is minimum for most desks.

Other important components of a study center include convenient book storage, properly located convenience outlets for such items as radio, electric typewriter, tape deck, etc., and a source of fresh air.

Redwood for a Study Wall

Consider redwood (or other type of wood) lumber paneling for one wall of a teenager's room. The paneling is sound-absorbing, which is a decided advantage. It may also add resale value to your house...or be an attractive surface should you convert this room into your own study once the kids are on their own.

To cover one wall and create a study center large enough for two, follow the instructions and photos on pages 52 and 53. For larger projects and more inventive applications, write to the California Redwood Association for their pamphlet on construction tips for paneling a room.

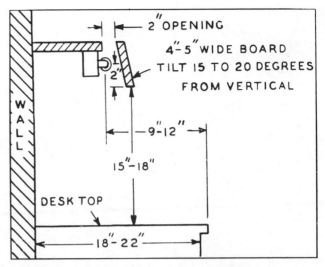

Side view of an easy-to-build desk fluorescent shelf shows the proper location as basic construction details. The unit as drawn here is without end panel to conceal framing and fluorescent tube. (Drawing courtesy of General Electric.)

It took less than a day to assemble this cabinet-shelf-desk combination for a ▶ child's room. Pegs in the end wall provide hanging storage and the desk is topped with plastic laminate. Shelves at right are fixed in place while those in the cabinet can be adjusted in height. (Instructions follow on page 50) (Photo courtesy of Western Wood Products Assn.)

Study Center

When purchasing lumber, please remember that actual widths and depths are slightly less than stock measurements. A 1x10 stock board, for example, is actually ¾"x9½". In this book, all total width and depth measurements in inches are actual.

1 Pre-cut all pieces as listed on page 3, squaring ends.

Unit A: Pre-drill screw holes in upright dividers, placing holes 4¾" from top and bottom edges. Drill two holes for coat hanger dowels. Cut shelf tracks to 32" and screw onto dividers 6" apart. (Figure 1-A) Construct unit with glue, screws and grommets.

Unit B: Glue and nail as per figure 1-B.

Unit C: Pre-drill screw holes in dividers as located in Figure 1-C. Construct unit. Hint: when affixing permanent shelves, pre-drill screw holes ½" into end of shelf to prevent splitting.

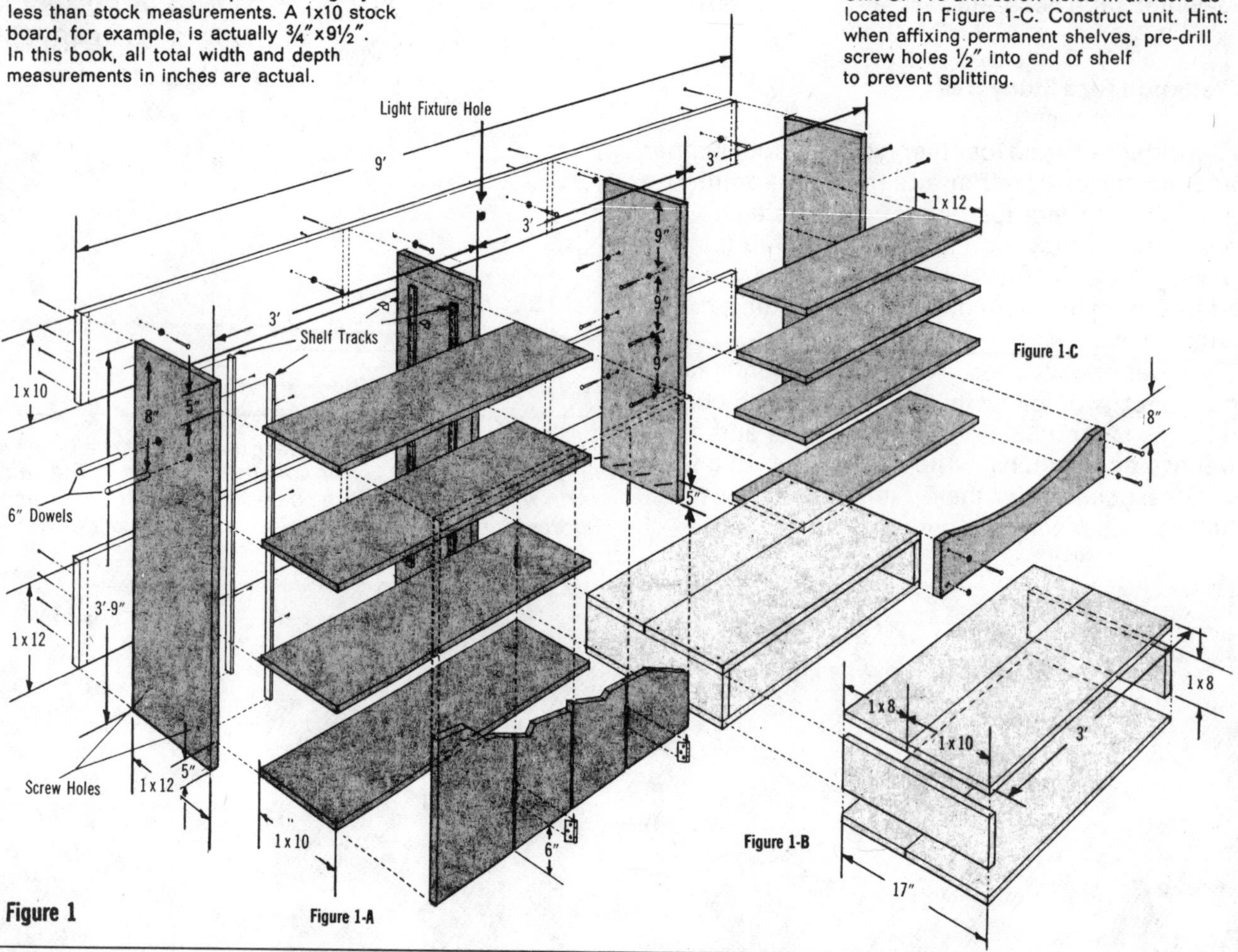

Light Fixture Hole

9'

3'

1 x 12

Figure 1-C

3'

9"

8"

Shelf Tracks

1 x 10

8"

5"

9"

6" Dowels

5"

3'-9"

1 x 12

5"

1 x 8

1 x 8

1 x 10

3'

Screw Holes

1 x 12

5"

1 x 10

6"

Figure 1-B

17"

Figure 1

Figure 1-A

2

Place units A and C face down on floor (Figure 2) gluing and nailing backboards flush across tops and bottoms. Be sure space allotted Unit B is 3 feet.

3

Construct doors as shown in Figure 4, attaching A hinges where indicated. Measure and drill hinge B screw holes on dividers. Attach B hinges to doors. Do not attach doors to dividers until entire unit is mounted on wall.

To mount on wall, locate studs and drill backboard for screws or bolts. (To aid stud location, remember studs are generally placed on 16" centers.) If studs or other solid support are not available, use toggle bolts (Figure 3).

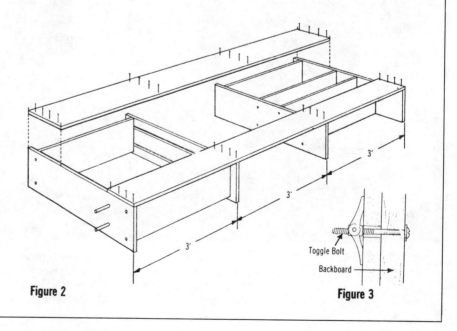

3'

3'

3'

Toggle Bolt

Backboard

Figure 2

Figure 3

4

Support unit to desired height and attach to wall. Recommended clearance from bottom of lower shelves to floor: children ages 5 to 12, 18″ to 24″; adults, 26″ to 28″.

Mount unit B by drilling, gluing and screwing through sides of Units A and C. Bottom of desk should be flush with bottom of A's lower shelf.

5

Using a wooden yardstick, scribe an arc (Figure 5) and cut bin front with keyhole or jig saw. Drill and attach with screws and grommets flush with bottom of desk (1-C).

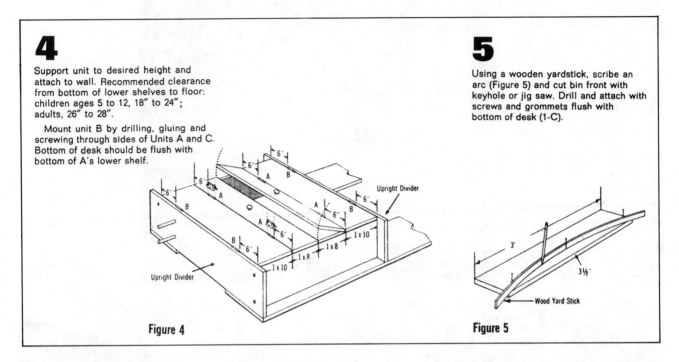

Figure 4

Figure 5

Materials list:

Backboards:	1 piece 1″ x 10″ x 9′
	1 piece 1″ x 12″ x 9′
Upright Dividers:	4 pieces 1″ x 12″ x 3′-9″
Shelves:	4 pieces 1″ x 10″ x 2′-10½″
	4 pieces 1″ x 12″ x 2′-10½″
Doors:	2 pieces 1″ x 10″ x 3′
	2 pieces 1″ x 8″ x 3′
Bin Front:	1 piece 1″ x 8″ x 3′
Bin Bottom:	1 piece 1″ x 12″ x 2′-10½″
Desk Sides:	2 pieces 1″ x 6″ x 1′-5″
Desk Top:	1 piece 1″ x 8″ x 3′
	1 piece 1″ x 10″ x 3′
Desk Bottom:	1 piece 1″ x 8″ x 3′
	1 piece 1″ x 10″ x 3′
Dowels:	2 pieces ¾″ x 6″
Bulletin Board:	Cork or fiberboard 2′ x 3′
Shelf Hardware:	4 pieces shelf standard 3′
	24 shelf supports
Door Hardware:	8 butt hinges 1½″ x ¾″
	2 wood door pulls
	2 catches (friction or magnetic)
Screws & Grommets:	3 dozen No. 10 rnd. head 1½″
	wood screws (bright finish)
	3 dozen bright finish grommets
Glue:	2 fluid ounces white glue
Toggles (if needed):	6 toggle bolts 2½″

6

Mount bulletin board on wall using screws and grommets or strong adhesives. Mount doors, pulls and catches. Glue and insert dowel coat hangers. Install light and insert adjustable shelves. Finish as desired.

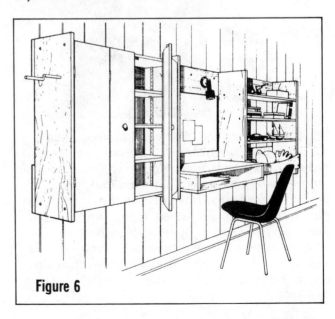

Figure 6

Before

After

Redwood
for a
Study Wall

Tools and materials Redwood lumber paneling (Certified Kiln Dried, Clear All Heart or Clear Grade); redwood baseboard, molding, trim, nails (finishing or casing nails for most paneling); adhesive, clearly marked for interior paneling; caulking gun; sandpaper; stain, sealer, thinner, brushes, etc.; hammer; saws (crosscut, rip and keyhole or sabre saw); carpenter's square, try square; tape measure; nail set; level or plumb line; block plane, screwdrivers; wood rasp; laminated desk top; shelving and brackets.

Steps

1. *Determine lumber needed. Trim is measured by linear foot. Add to wall requirements sufficient baseboard molding for desk front. Add ceiling molding to finish back and sides of desktop and an equal amount to use as cleats to support desk top. To determine amount of lumber needed for paneling, determine the square footage of your walls and convert this to board and linear feet of lumber, using the conversion factors provided by the California Redwood Association.*

   First multiply each wall's total width by its height and subtract non-paneled areas, windows and doors.

Then multiply this figure by the board and linear foot conversion factors appropriate for the width of your lumber. Paneling 100 square feet of wall space with 6 in. side lumber requires 115 board ft. (100 x 1.15 = 115) or 230 linear ft. (115 x 2 = 230). Be sure to allow 5% extra for errors and end trim loss.

2. Store redwood lumber for several days away from moisture, direct sunlight and heat vents, preferably in the room to be paneled.

3. Remove all outlet and switch plates (tape screws to each to avoid losing them), and hot and cold air duct covers. If you want to extend outlet boxes for added paneling thickness, shut off electricity at the fuse panel beforehand. Outlets also may be left neatly recessed. As individual boards go up, cut openings, measuring from the adjoining board and from the floor or ceiling. Mark dimensions in the panel face; drill four large holes just inside marked corners, and saw from them with a sabre or keyhole saw.

4. Arrange lumber before you glue paneling, creating most attractive variations from one board to next. Begin vertical paneling at an inside corner. Work left to right if you are right-handed, right to left if left-handed. Keep groove edges toward the starting corner, and tongue edges toward your work direction. Trial fit the first board and check for plumb, then nail with 5d or 6d finishing nails, even if other boards are to be glued on.

5. Measure all other boards carefully and trial fit. Tap them into place with a hammer and tapping block, a scrap with the groove edge intact to fit over board tongues. Check for plumb, and, if necessary, slightly angle groove-to-groove fitting to make it square. When butt joining short board ends together in the middle of a wall, be sure the joint falls over a stud, blocking or furring strip.

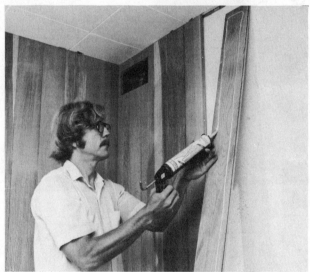

6. To glue panels, apply adhesive generously with caulking gun to the back of a prefitted board. Let it set according to adhesive package directions, then hold board to wall so both are coated. Remove it, wait again, then tap the board into place and face-nail top and bottom with 8d finishing nails (two nails at each end for wider boards). During waiting periods, you can finish one board while adhesive sets on another.

7. The last board may have to be trimmed to fit into a corner. Angle trim the board's corner edge slightly, with a block plane, with the wide part of the angle toward the wall.

8. To install redwood moldings and baseboards, measure floors and ceilings separately. Miter join molding and baseboard ends on outside corners, and butt join them on inside corners.

9. Finish wall as desired.

10. To make study area, use plastic laminated desktop or, if area is small enough, a flush door. Install shelf brackets and redwood planks for use as shelving. (Note: you can use single-groove fascia for shelving and allow the bracket front end to fit into the groove for the free-floating effect of shelving in illustration, where bracket heads do not show.

11. *Set desk top at 26 in. height for greatest comfort. Nail ceiling molding around sides and back where desk will be attached underneath as a support. Use "L" brackets to attach legs made from redwood plank or fascia to desk top from underneath. Nail desk top to supporting molding cleats.*

12. *Finish desk top by nailing on ceiling molding around back edge and sides, into wall instead of desk top. Finish front edge with baseboard molding, flush with desk top and overhanging below desk. Finish desk and shelving redwood to match wall finish.*

BASEMENTS

Homeowners with children have found the basement an excellent place to gain valuable living area at minimum cost, often doubling the usable floor area of a home. Depending upon the age of the children who will use this space, the basement can literally "grow" with the youngsters as they progress from building blocks to teenage dancing parties.

To many, the basement has long been a catch-all for a lot of things that worked their way from frequent to infrequent usage. Often this ready-to-improve space has been plagued with dampness, poor lighting and total lack of decoration, unless you enjoy gazing at ceiling plumbing or heating pipes and ducts.

Preplanning your basement space for children's

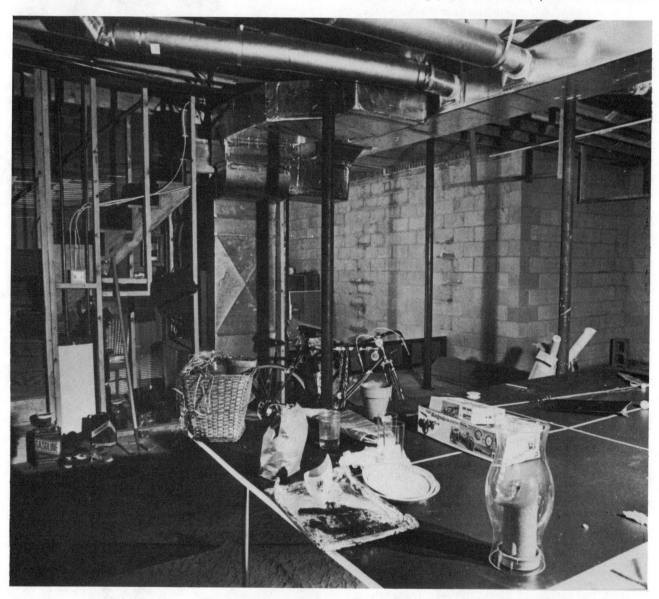

Before remodeling, this unfinished basement was the "catch all" for a typical family's paraphernalia. With careful planning and do-it-yourself enthusiasm, it evolved into a cozy, versatile space suitable for a variety of activities by all members of the family.

use needn't be complicated or overly elaborate. Begin with a floor plan that sectionalizes the total area according to the specific uses you desire. Frequently these will include separate spaces for heating and storage, laundry, workshop, game room, TV room, and recreation or playroom.

Combatting Excess Moisture

Assuming that you will want to use these spaces all year, you must initially handle the problem of summer condensation of moisture from the air. This problem occurs when warm, moist air from the outdoors comes in contact with cool basement walls and floors, and with uninsulated cold water pipes. The water then condenses on the cool surfaces. Dampness caused by condensation can usually be cured by warming the basement through either ventilation, insulation, or extension of heating—or by reduction of the amount of moisture in the basement by dehumidifying. By opening basement windows in dry weather, the walls and floors can be warmed in the summer. An exhaust fan installed in a basement window and operated during the day is helpful in circulating air through the basement. However, ventilation alone is not a very dependable cure for moisture problems. Waterproofing paint can be part of your solution, although it is frequently

By building a boxed beam and enclosing a steel post, an attractive dining nook was created (upper right). The breakfast/snack bar is delineated with fluorescent lighting integrated in the suspended acoustical ceiling, and hides overhead pipes and ducts. Walls are covered with paneling concealing fuse boxes and plumbing. (Photo courtesy Armstrong Cork Co.)

Accommodating a standard-size fold-up table-tennis table, an open area at one end of the basement also holds a Peg-Board storage wall with overhead fluorescent illumination. The vinyl flooring has a cushion back for comfort. (Photo Courtesy Armstrong Cork Co.)

not sufficient in itself.

The amount of moisture in a basement can be reduced by a mechanical dehumidifier, which extracts the moisture and deposits it in a tank or allows it to run down the drain. The mechanical dehumidifier is essentially a small refrigeration unit, and the moisture in the air condenses on the coils since they are colder than any other surface in the basement. Some heat is given off in the operation of a dehumidifier, which further helps to control condensation.

Walls can be kept above the temperature of the ground by the use of insulation. When the walls are warmer, the moisture in the air will not condense readily on them. Moisture-resistant insulation and a built-in vapor barrier must be used. To reduce the amount of water that collects on cold water pipes,

insulate them with foamed or wrapped insulation.

DECORATIVE POSSIBILITIES

Whitewash no longer is the standard decor for basements. Pastel colors are available in long-lasting portland cement base paints that can provide many decorative schemes. In addition, hundreds of different prefinished wood and hardwood panelings are available from local retail lumber dealers for use in the basement.

Partitions

Walls dividing basements into specific-use areas need not be load-bearing in design and thus are easier for the homeowner to construct. Such partitions are easily attached to concrete floor surfaces with power stud drivers, while top plates are simply nailed to the overhead floor joist. Electrical wiring can be easily strung in the overhead areas and along studs of the new partitions to provide for convenience outlets and wall switches.

Sound Control

Sound conditioning is an important phase of construction in creating basement space for children. The two key areas, of course, being floor and ceiling.

Do-it-yourself materials on the market make it a relatively easy job to install a suspended acoustical ceiling that will reduce noise levels and hide unsightly pipes and ducts. Such ceilings with "lay in" panels and metal grid system frequently are designed to also accommodate luminous ceiling lighting panels that eliminate the need for hanging fixtures. (See also Chapter 7.)

Floors

Basement floors (below grade) may be covered with special grades of resilient flooring, carpeting and wood-finish flooring. Uneven floors can be made level by using 2 x 4 inch sleepers and shims to create a totally new floor surface.

Windows

Most basements are constructed with small, hopper-style windows that open from the top and have an all-glass area of approximately 7 feet above the floor level. Such windows frequently are totally out of scale with finished-room decorating schemes and thus require special treatment to visually put them in scale. Small, high windows can be hidden with decorative blinds or window coverings that give the appearance of shielding full-size windows when closed. Curtain rods that extend to each side, or that fall below the bottom edge, will give this illusion. Generally speaking, these windows rarely need to be opened and therefore can be treated as totally fixed windows.

You might also consider creating false window fronts. Artificial windows can be built in with backlighting and an opaque sheet that diffuses light to simulate sunlight. For the best results, such windows should be installed in paneled walls with sufficient depth to accommodate an artificial window. Semi-transparent curtains or shutters will allow just a hint of the artificial sunlight to shine in.

Built-in redwood shelves and cabinets are attached to a wall of 1 x 6 redwood clear all-heart paneling. The raised bed platform simplifies vacuuming and has a convenient headboard divider for tuner, turntable, record storage and telephone. (Photo courtesy of California Redwood Assn.)

6
Storage

"A place for everything and everything in its place" may be an old saying, but it's also a near impossibility when it comes to a child's room.

CLOSETS

In the author's opinion, the room's closet is the most important storage facility for a child, yet it's always provided by the builder for adult use. How you change this storage will greatly affect what's "left over" at the end of the day or following a "go-clean-your-room session".

The first change that should be made in the closet is to put at least one bar at the child's height. And since most children don't have an exceptionally large "in season" wardrobe, part of the width of the closet at this lower level can be fitted with removable box-style compartments into which shoes, toys, games and other items can be placed by the young-

"Dial-A-Closet" fittings produced by Wessel Hardware Corp. and sold throughout the country by local hardware and lumber dealers permit you to increase hanging space in a closet by more than 50% and more than double the existing shelf space. Combinations of the various components fit any closet ranging from 29" to 121" wide.

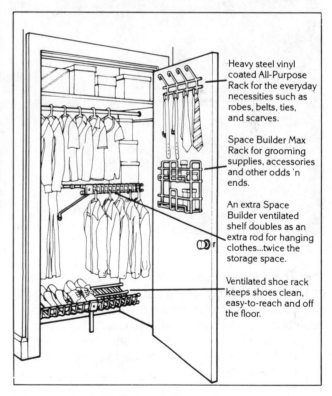

Heavy steel vinyl coated All-Purpose Rack for the everyday necessities such as robes, belts, ties, and scarves.

Space Builder Max Rack for grooming supplies, accessories and other odds 'n ends.

An extra Space Builder ventilated shelf doubles as an extra rod for hanging clothes...twice the storage space.

Ventilated shoe rack keeps shoes clean, easy-to-reach and off the floor.

Closet space can accommodate twice the usual contents when arranged in orderly fashion. This drawing shows Space Builder ventilated shelving made of vinyl-coated steel rods.

A small-space bedroom for a teenager or college student can still offer order with a minimum cash outlay. This tiny room has wall-hung desk with pedestal drawer units and an open ledge to hold all paper supplies. The room is paneled with flush-joint western hemlock boards finished clear. Shelves are adjustable, the bottom one equipped with fluorescent lighting strips. Woven wood blinds fit within the window frames. (Photo courtesy of Western Wood Products Assn.)

An extra bedroom was converted to a den-study-storage area in this home. Western cedar V-joint 6-in. boards were used for the walls and matching doors which enclose the television and under-eave closet for toys, games, etc. A small desk is surrounded by fixed-in-place bookshelves.

ster. The original closet bar can be retained for "out of season" clothing, or the bar simply removed and more cubicle and shelf space provided with a lower cubicle box provided as a step to reach this area.

In addition to the bedroom closet, storage space for children's belongings can be located in other areas of the house.

Bedroom Storage

Under the bed Use low-height boxes, a plywood panel on casters, drawers or small boxes to store infrequently-used items.

In the headboard Many beds come with compartments that can be used for book and other storage. Some headboards also have shelf-type tops that can be used for radio, clock, lamp, etc.

Around the headboard Custom arrangements are numerous for making this a working storage wall.

Hanging baskets Use chain or rope to suspend various-sized baskets from the ceiling for easy in-and-out storage.

Inside swinging closet doors Tie racks are most familiar in an adult bedroom, but the same space can be used for any number of child items. Small boxes and shelves with "guard" rails prove most handy.

Footlockers That old college trunk or army footlocker placed at the foot of the bed provides closed storage for toys, games, and other childhood "treasures".

Dividerwalls When used to create separate sleeping areas for two or more youngsters, these partitions can be equipped with drawers and shelves.

Plywood or particleboard faced with plain-color or woodgrain plastic laminate can be used to make floor-to-ceiling storage walls in the home. This unit is slightly less than ceiling height so that it is portable; it was assembled in two sections. (Photo courtesy of Formica Corp.)

Raggedy Ann and Andy wall plaque for a tots room is 22 x 14 in. and comes with five white pegs for hanging up little jackets, overalls, hats, etc. (Photo courtesy of Syroco).

Home hallways can be put to storage use with the easy addition of shelves and cabinets, maximizing locations where children's items can be kept. (Photo courtesy of Western Wood Products Assn.)

Bathroom Storage

Around-the-toilet   Most bath specialty stores offer a selection of floor-to-ceiling storage units that can be quickly installed around a toilet and used for bath items. Still other units are designed for hanging on the wall, directly over the toilet tank to make use of this otherwise-wasted space.

On the bathtub   If you are selecting a new tub, consider one that has an integral shelf for bath soaps, cosmetics, water toys, etc.

Lavatory-vanity unit   Wall-hung lavatories are the least expensive bathroom fixtures, but have become less desirable with the widespread use of vanities that provide floor-to-bowl storage space.

Modular furniture available for children's rooms presents countless ways in which convenient storage can be assembled and then changed as needs change. This arrangement incorporates Schoolfield Furniture Industries' platform bed and "700 Swingers" storage units. (Photo courtesy of Syroco.)

Hanging shelf units Wood, plastic and aluminum-frame hanging shelf arrangements available at many department stores can be suspended on the outside of sliding bathtub-shower doors or on the end wall opposite bathtub faucets.

Corner what-nots Triangular corner what-not shelves take up little space in a bathroom and yet permit open storage of much-used items such as bath salts, bubble bath, etc.

See also: Successful Bathrooms by Joseph Schram.

See also: Chapter 4.

General Storage

Window seats Many newer homes built with window seats are framed in such a way that removal of facing wallboard provides a new under-window storage area.

Between studs Narrow-depth shelf storage can generally be easily installed between studs once the wall surfacing has been removed. Such areas in unfinished garages are good locations for storing baseball bats, skis, archery sets, etc.

Under stairways Some builders originally provide this storage area, but in homes where they don't, removal of wallboard and installation of access doors provide excellent storage for child use.

Room dividers Space on either side of a wall usually can be converted to a storage-style room divider, with shelf and cabinet space designed specifically for your storage needs including stereo equipment, tape decks, record storage, TV, books, etc. Plans for constructing these units are offered by most building material dealers.

Room corners Furniture-finish kitchen cabinets offered in most major lines include special cabinets for corner use, either as wall or base style.

See also: Successful Shelves & Built-ins by Jay Hedden.

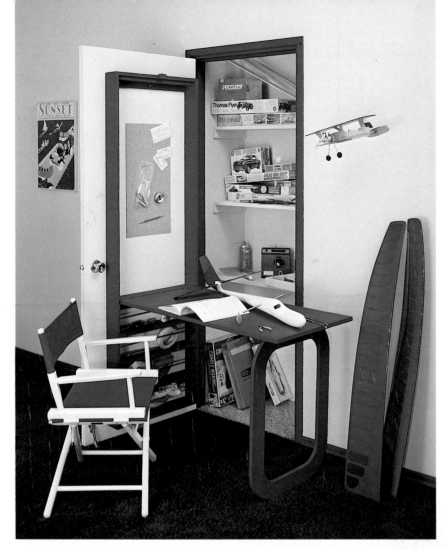

A work space where none existed! And a great way to avoid the clutter of a child's on going project. This easy to build unit folds out of a standard closet and plans are available from the American Plywood Association. (Photo courtesy of the American Plywood Association)

In many older homes rooms still exist without the closet space that so many children now require. This complete unit acts as bunk beds, closet and dresser. Note that the steps to the top bunk can also be used for storage. (Photo courtesy of the American Plywood Association and plans for this project are available from the American Plywood Association)

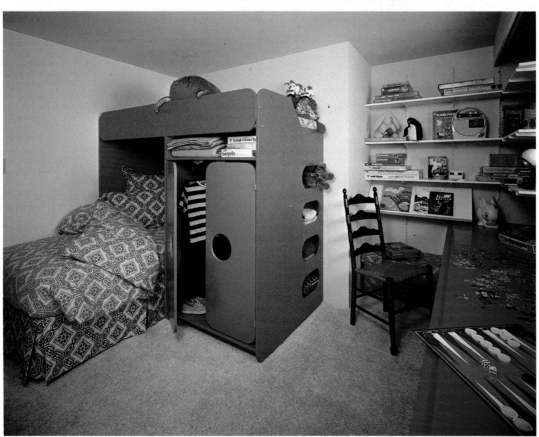

The private and/or secret world of childhood is beautifully staged by this sleep-in, play-in, study-in bedroom for two small boys, or girls. The tent is made of natural color, painter's Belgian linen canvas and is complete with two folding army cots, folding mattresses, down comforters, portable camp stools and battery-operated lights. Painted steel shelving is adjustable in one-inch increments. (Photo courtesy of the Belgian Linen Association)

Bedroom-playroom combinations can adopt many different themes including this pirate "ship" with corner crow's nest fashioned from a plain wooden barrel set atop a wooden mast and bordered on either side by clerestory windows. The room has resilient flooring for easy maintenance, acoustical ceiling for sound control and lots of built-in storage space for boy's treasures. Study space flanks the crow's nest and built-in bunk beds have been installed in such a way that one boy can go to sleep and not be disturbed while the other boy continues working at his desk. (Photo courtesy of the Armstrong Cork Co.)

◄ Designed for a "young salt", this seaworthy room combines easy-care carpeting, self-stick floor tiles, a wood plank ceiling, new furniture and clever accessorizing in a marine motif. The flexible furniture pieces are from Thomasville's Pine Manor Collection and feature a trundle bed and corner desk. (Photo courtesy of the Armstrong Cork Co.)

Children's storage can be provided in a variety of ways conducive to getting them to use it on a regular basis. Here simple wicker bicycle baskets are suspended from a decorative drapery rod to catch stuffed animals and other toys. A larger wicker basket with cover adds foot locker storage. Use of resilient flooring permits easy clean up of spilled or misdirected water paints. (Photo courtesy of the Armstrong Cork Co.)

Ventilated vinyl-coated steel rods are key to the design of Space Builder storage units by Closet Maid Corp. This type of storage space prevents rust, mold, mildew and musty odors.

A single bunk with plenty of play storage and high sides is the perfect "first bunk" for your growing child. Easy to build plans from American Plywood along with your child's imagination can make this a combination play/ sleep area without using much floor space. (Photo courtesy of the American Plywood Association)

Well-planned built-ins can help to eliminate clutter in a child's room. This open-shelf unit provides desk space as well as a four-shelf cabinet with accordion-hinged doors. The off-the-floor arrangement simplifies floor cleaning. (Photo courtesy of the Western Wood Products Assn.)

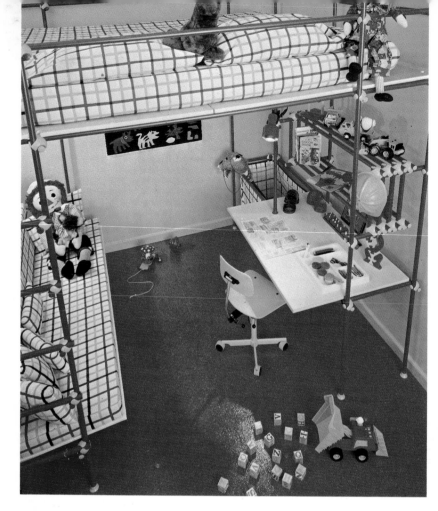

A small-space bedroom can be made more useful with furniture that hooks together like a giant tinkertoy. The tubular system used here takes little space, yet affords seating, desk play and bunk sleeping. The exuberant multi-colored plaid fabric picks up colors of floor, wall and furniture. (Photo courtesy of the GAF Corp.)

Create this economical desk for the student at home with only two file cabinets and one sheet of formica or painted plywood. The bunk beds are built in and plans are available from the American Plywood Association. (Photo courtesy of the American Plywood Association)

Eight panels of strippable-scrubbable wallcovering were used to create this aquarium scene by Environmental Graphics, Inc. The material allows for 8'8" height and 13'8" width.

GAF Corp. designers created this total environment unit for two children that you can build with plywood. Included in the unit are desk, two 75"x30" bunk beds, shelves for games and a long storage unit under the stairs. Sheet vinyl used for the floor and stairs adds contrast to the solid enamel paint colors.

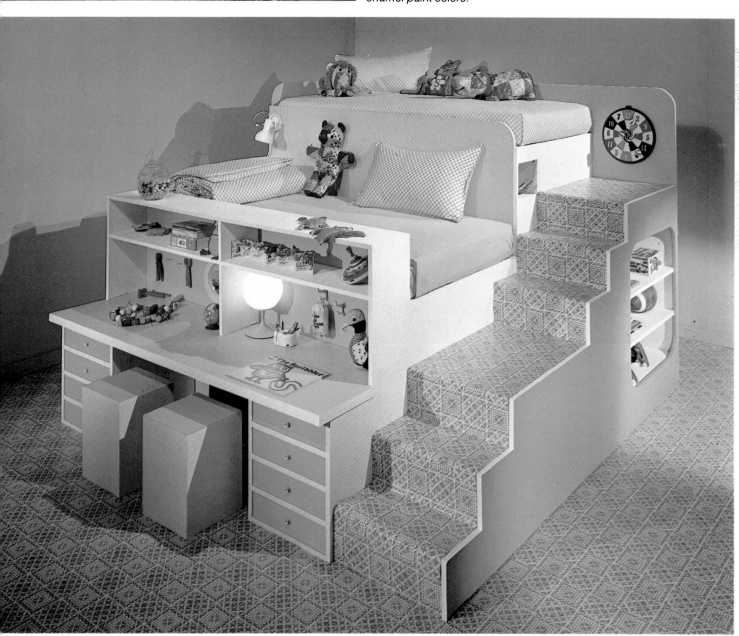

Open cabinets are provided along the back wall and half way along side walls to accommodate a child's interests at any age. Deep peach carpeting was installed over resilient tile and aluminum blinds added at the window to control light and heat. Child-level furniture was replaced in the teenage setting by adult-style chest and seating. The fabric and wallpaper are "Pricilla's Fancy" by Albert Van Luit.

7
Basics for Noise Control & Lighting

SOUND SYSTEMS

Hi-Fi and Stereo

Most parents are interested in having their children develop an appreciation of music, and thus will attempt to expose them to quality music at an early age.

Telling someone what to purchase in high fidelity or stereo is like picking out a suit for someone else —there is an excellent chance it won't fit; it will be the wrong color or style and it will remain in the closet. Teenagers especially should have the opportunity to select the music system that pleases their ears, if not yours.

Most young children begin their music enjoyment with a simple phonograph. They merely plug it into the wall and plop a record in place, with only the sound volume knob as a control. This "toy" soon is replaced with perhaps a clock-radio offering AM-FM bands. Then comes the hi-fi system, and the adult need for earplugs.

Acquisition of a hi-fi system, whether it is a set that is mass-manufactured or custom-made, depends on proper electronic ingredients, wisely selected and skillfully balanced. Also the acquisition depends absolutely on the ear of the buyer.

In buying, he should be prepared to exercise the most sensitive judgement, particularly if he has an untrained or easily satisfied ear. For as one's ear grows in sensitivity, the hi-fi set one acquired at an early stage may become less than satisfying.

Learn to listen for the varying characters of loud speakers, for example. They reflect an almost human diversity—some are mellow, others brilliant in tone. There is excitement, no doubt, in the sheer volume of sound, even in noise. Hence careless listeners fall for the temptation of a loud system.

Before you buy, sample the sounds and check your taste against your budget. You can acquire a system as a "package" unit or through the use of components. The package variety is an appliance-type, radio phonograph, tape deck combination usually sold in consoles.

Components are separate building blocks of a high-fidelity sound system, the basic components of which are a turntable, amplifier and loud speaker. You can add a radio tuner, tape recorder-player and additional speakers for stereo arrangement. Usually each component is made by a different manufacturer. He concentrates his energies in building the finest unit he can. Components have several advantages:

- They fit easily into any room or decor, and can be either permanently built-in or put into anything from a bookcase to a table—or be placed in specially built cabinets.
- Component systems can be assembled step by step. You don't have to buy them all at once. You can start with the essentials and add other units later. Also, your system can be upgraded piece by piece.

A basic understanding of high fidelity is most important in making your selections. The first link of the system is a record changer or separate turntable and arm. It rotates a record and brings it in contact with the cartridge, a small sensitive device that traces the sound vibrations engraved in the record, converting them to electrical signals.

The second link, the amplifier, is the nerve center of your music system. It receives the tiny electrical impulses from a phono cartridge, radio tuner or tape recorder and amplifies them until they are strong enough to drive a high fidelity loudspeaker system. Amplifiers are sometimes divided into two parts: the pre-amplifier containing all the controls and the power amplifier which produces the loudspeaker driving power from the signal supplied by the pre-amplifier.

73

The final link is the loudspeaker, which converts electrical signals from the amplifier back into the audible sound vibrations and projects the sound into the room.

In selecting a home music system it is well to have at least a general knowledge of the differences involved in high fidelity, stereo, and stereo quadraphonic. High-fidelity refers to the quality of reproduction. Stereophonic and stereo quadraphonic are methods. Actually, stereo may be high or low fidelity.

Early radios and phonographs with their coarsely cut 78 rpm recordings reproduced a narrow range of tones. Background and surface noises gave distortion, and instruments often blurred together in nerve-wracking jangle.

High fidelity   Designed to reproduce music free of distortion and outside noise, high fidelity endeavors to present every note and its overtones in exactly the same form, intensity and character as its live counterpart.

Stereo   Two-dimensional, it arises from the fact that our ears receive sound waves from two sides. Sound is heard by one ear a little later than the other, with slightly different intensity and phasing. With monophonic sound, in which music comes from one loudspeaker, dimensional characteristics are lost. For stereophonic sound, music is recorded by two microphones placed a few feet apart. Sound from each microphone is transcribed separately. Each track or channel is reproduced separately but simultaneously and projected through two speakers. This permits us to hear the dimension of music— the width of a symphony orchestra, the depth of a stage, the individual placement and movement of soloists.

Stereo quadraphonic   This fairly recent innovation provides full, richer concert-hall sound by using all four channels of stereo records, tape recordings and special radio presentations. Four-channel sound is offered in three types: regular matrix, SQ and discrete. Regular matrix doesn't have as much separation as SQ, while discrete provides excellent tonal quality reproduction and entirely distinct sound separation.

Most stereo buffs and experts will tell you that you get exactly what you pay for when it comes to selecting equipment. It's always wise to buy the best equipment you can pay for, and to be certain the units have the capability of "adding-to" so you can upgrade with components that are "compatible" with your original purchases.

Acoustical Ceiling Tiles

If ever a product were invented with children in mind, it has to be acoustical ceiling material. The noise coefficient of children runs from never-zero to immeasurable, and the use of acoustical material on the ceilings of their rooms has become a marvelous blood-pressure control for parents.

Home noise increases each year: hi-fi units become more powerful; more appliances (hair blowers, etc.) are put in use; air conditioners are added. The eardrums of parents take a constant pounding.

Psychologists have found that it is not always the volume and variety of noises that can heighten nervous tension, but rather the frame of mind of the listener. Men in boiler factories work all day battered by ear splitting sounds and suffer little more than slight hearing loss. But unexpected jarring sounds at home can raise blood pressures and tempers. It appears that while people who work around loud and predictable noises grow accustomed to them, people expect peace and quiet at home.

Use of carpets and drapes, and correct placement of furniture, can also help to insulate your home from outside noise and cut down some of the acoustical distractions of an active family. But one of the biggest causes of noisy interiors is a smooth, hard ceiling that causes sound waves to bounce back into the room. A large percentage of sound waves from a hi-fi speaker, for example, bounce off ceilings just fractions of a second after the listener hears the direct waves. This causes a boomy effect, which not only detracts from the quality of the recorded sound but also can be annoying to family members in other rooms.

A ceiling covered with acoustical material can absorb up to 70 percent of the sound striking it. You can choose from materials that are affixed directly to the ceiling surface, or suspended units that give a dropped ceiling effect.

Acoustical and decorative ceiling tiles have improved dramatically from a visual standpoint. Units with precisely squared edges on all four sides fit snugly against one another to form a continuous, unbroken surface. And the new manufacturing process permits highly sophisticated embossing on the tile face, opening up a galaxy of appealing designs and styles.

Installation of tile ceilings has been simplified to the point where almost any homeowner can handle the job with common household tools. Armstrong's Intergrid system, for example, does away with cutting and nailing of wood furring strips, and doesn't require stapling. Lightweight channels (or runners)

The first step: nail Intergrid furring channels at 4-ft. intervals spanning the width of the room.

Metal molding is nailed around perimeter of room, approximately 2 in. below the level of the existing ceiling.

The new channels are designed to receive Intergrid cross tees which, in turn, support ceiling tiles. To attach, bend the sides of the channels slightly inward and clip on the tee. The cross tee should slide easily along the length of the channel.

Lay the first row of tiles on the wall molding, then slide the cross tee forward until it is engaged in a concealed slot in the leading edges of the tiles. This completes installation of the first row.

Continue across the room in this manner, installing tiles and cross tees.

At the completion of each row, a metal tension spring is inserted between the wall and the last tile in order to hold the seams tightly together. This prevents separation of tiles due to movement of the building.

are simply attached (or hung) from the existing ceiling, and the tiles are held in place with supporting cross tees which snap into place. The supporting gridwork then is completely hidden from view in the finished ceiling.

The Intergrid system accommodates either 12 x 12 inch tiles or larger 1 x 4 feet units, and requires a 2 inch drop from the existing ceiling. A recessed fluorescent light fixture is also offered with the system, or the system also can be used with conventional hanging light fixtures.

LIGHTING

No room—for child or adult—can be properly planned and decorated without proper lighting. Just as air conditioning provides year-round comfort, adequate lighting adds to visual comfort, prevents eye damage, and provides living flexibility.

Adequate Lighting

Lighting actually begins even before a fixture is installed, for every surface reflects some of the natural light it receives. Light can be absorbed by dark surfaces, or reflected by light surfaces and utilized as useful illumination.

General Electric lighting specialists who have devoted lifelong careers to proper home illumination stress that proper lighting begins with recommended reflectances for major surfaces. Ceilings should be pale color tints that reflect a minimum 60 percent to a maximum 90 percent; walls should be medium shades that reflect from 35 to 60 percent; and floors of carpeting, tile or wood should reflect from 15 to 35 percent.

The reflectance levels of these major surfaces and the amount of light they receive form the backgrounds against which most visual activity takes place. They are always, whether we are aware of them or not, somewhere within our field of view. As a consequence our visual comfort, mental attitude, and emotional mood is influenced by the balance that exists between the sources of illumination, the items to be seen, and the backgrounds against which they are viewed.

Research has proven that modern home living requires three basic types of illumination: general or fill-in lighting of 5 to 10 footcandles; local or functional lighting for specific visual tasks; and, accent or decorative lighting. Of these three, by far the most important is specific task lighting, which may range from a minimum 10 footcandles for card games to 200 footcandles for hobbies with small details.

With the wealth of data readily available to builders, architects, interior designers and homeown-

Lighting is a key decorating tool in this basement turned "Rathskeller". The relaxation area has a recessed downlight that highlights the round table while three adjustable eyeball fixtures, on dimmer, are aimed to light the music rack of the antique piano and wall behind.
The adjacent area is used for dancing and has a series of downlights containing pink and blue-white reflector lamps that are on dimmer for flexibility of lighting level. (Photo courtesy of General Electric)

General lighting in a child's bedroom is provided here by a fluorescent bracket above the closet doors. The unit contains two 40-watt warm-white tubes which are shielded on the bottom by a diffuser. The general lighting provides 5 to 10 footcandles throughout the room and 10 footcandles at the closet. (Photo courtesy of General Electric)

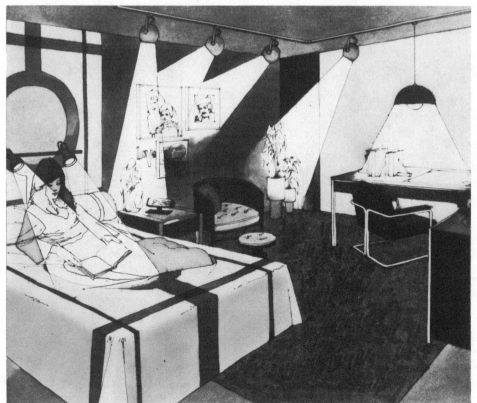

Track lighting systems permit you to move the individual units to the exact spot you wish. You can bathe a wall, a drapery, an entire area with light, or you can illuminate a reading or work area in the manner that is most helpful. Track lights are mounted to the ceiling or wall in an electrified track that provides current over as extensive an area as you wish. (Photo courtesy of Lightcraft of California, a NuTone Div.)

The lighted canopy above the mirror contains two 40-watt warm-white fluorescent lamps, channel-mounted to the ceiling and centered over the diffuser for good grooming. The lighted canopy in the tub area has one 40-watt warm-white fluorescent. Total bath lighting is 182 watts, an energy-saving feature. (Photo courtesy of General Electric)

Two teenage girls share this bathroom which has twin lavatories and a lighted soffit–an efficient means of lighting at the mirror and general room lighting. Two rows of 40-watt warm-white fluorescents are used, along with three 50R20's located elsewhere in the room. (Photo courtesy of General Electric)

ers alike, there is no excuse today for inadequate lighting, especially in children's rooms where young eyes can be so easily damaged. Today's fixtures are both decorative and functional. They are related to the space, integrated with the furnishings, and can be planned to serve changing activity.

Selection

Ceiling lighting fixtures may be surface-mounted, pendant or recessed. Wall units can be placed in a cornice for downlighting only, used as valance lighting both upward and downward, or mounted on the wall surface for both upward and downward lighting. Portable lamps can provide light over an area 40 to 50 feet, with about five portable units required for an average-sized room if it is lighted exclusively by this method.

Room Requirements

With children uppermost in mind, here's a brief rundown on lighting for specific areas they most inhabit at home:

Bedrooms   These areas require general lighting with a 3 to 5-socket ceiling-mounted or suspended fixture providing a total 150-200 watts; you can increase the fixture size in rooms over 150 square feet to provide 200 to 300 watts. If structural lighting is desired instead of ceiling unit, provide 8 to 12 foot-candles of illumination via valance, cornice or wall bracket. If a recessed unit is selected, two 40-watt fluorescent lamps should be used.

Bathrooms   Lighting at the mirror will illuminate the average-sized bathroom. Compartmented areas will require additional localized lighting. For small mirrors, use a set of three fixtures (one above, one on each side) wired to one switch. Each fixture should be shielded with wall brackets centered 30 inches apart, 60 inches above the floor. The ceiling unit should be centered over the front edge of the washbowl or counter—a minimum of 12 inches in diameter—with two 60-watt bulbs or two to four fluorescent tubes, 20-watt, 24 inches long. Large mirrors (36 inches or more in width) should have a double row of recessed deluxe warm white 30-watt, 36 inches, or 40-watt, 48 inches. Recommended soffit dimensions: 16 inches front-to-back; 8 inches deep; full length of counter. Mirrors also may be illuminated by theatrical-type units with exposed-lamp fixtures across top and sides of the mirror, four

to six 15-watt or 25-watt bulbs per strip. Separate compartments should have a minimum 75-watt R-30 recessed fixture, or 8 inches diameter 100-watt surface-mounted fixture or wall bracket. Showers and closed-in tubs should be illuminated with a recessed vapor-proof fixture for 75-watt or 100-watt, with switch outside of shower area. A 15-watt night light also is recommended.

Music Center   When the upright piano or organ is placed against a wall, recessed or surface-mounted adjustable fixture or track lighting should be located behind the user and aimed to cover music and immediate background. Bulbs should be 150 PAR floodlights. Placement should be 24 inches out from the center of the music rack for one bulb or same distance out and 30 inches to the left and right of the music rack for two bulbs. If a portable lamp is to be used it should have an open top, be of neutral color and have minimum dimensions of: top 10 inches, depth 10 inches and bottom 16 inches. The bulb should be a three-way 50/250-watt or 100/300-watt. Placement of the socket should be 13 inches in front of the lower edge of the music rack, and 22 inches to the right or left of the keyboard center.

Study Desk Area   Because of the great attention that should be given to this lighting function, this specific child center is covered in greater depth in Chapter 5.

Game & Hobby Areas   Permanent game tables should be illuminated with four 75-watt R-30 floodlights recessed or surface mounted, with fixtures placed two feet out diagonally from each corner of the table. Ping pong tables should have two surface-mounted, well-shielded 30-watt or two 40-watt fluorescent fixtures at each end of the table. Pool tables should have a recessed 150-watt, R-40 reflector floodlight centered over each half of the table. For carpentry or handicraft at a workbench, use an industrial reflector-type fixture with a minimum of two 40-watt cool white fluorescent tubes for 6-foot bench or pair of 150-watt silvered-bowl bulbs in reflectors spaced 3 feet apart. Placement should be over the front edge of the bench.

General Reading Requirements

Lighting engineers have established "minimums" for use of table, wall, and floor lamps in relation to reading while sitting in a chair or semi-reclined in bed. It should be remembered, however, that gen-

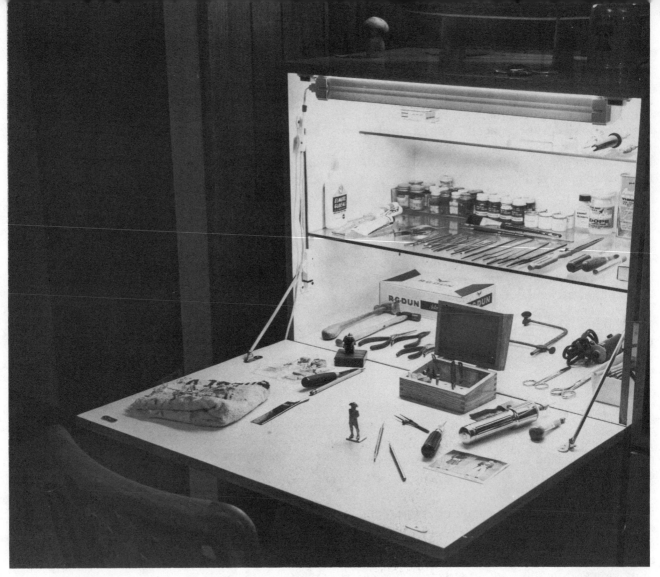

Working with tin is the hobby of the teenager who occupies this room. Excellent specific-task lighting is provided by a General Electric Bright Stik, a 25 in. fluorescent unit that needs no fixture or special wiring. It weighs 9 ounces and has its own cord, plug and switch.

eral illumination is a must in main areas used by children, for it appears most of their reading is done on the floor. Use of a table lamp for sit-down reading varies with the height of the table plus the lamp base height, but the major factor is keeping the 16-18 inch shade bottom approximately 40 inches from the floor and at eye level of the user. The bulb should be three-way 50/250 or 100/300-watt or soft white 150, 200, or 50/150-watt. Placement of the lamp should be with the center of the base about in line with the shoulder, and 20 inches left or right of the book center. Wall lamps are preferred for small rooms with furniture that is close to doors and windows. Recommended shade dimensions: top 6-8 inches; bottom 14-18 inches; depth 6-8 inches. Bulbs should be 100 to 150-watts and 50/250-watt multiple sockets

totaling 180-watts minimum (three 60-watt). Placement should be in line with the shoulder, centered 20 inches left or right of the center of the book, lower edge at eye level. If substantially behind the shoulder, center at 15 inches to the side with lower edge 47 to 49 inches above the floor.

Floor lamps should have a base height of 40 to 49 inches to the lower edge of the shade, in standard type and in double swing-arm, or single-arm bridge types. Bulbs should be 150 or 200-watt soft-white. For very low lamps (40 to 42 inches to shade bottom) place shaft in line with shoulder. For taller lamps, (40 to 42 inches to shade bottom) place shaft in line with shoulder. For taller lamps, (43 to 49 inches), place 15 inches left or right of book center and 26 inches back.

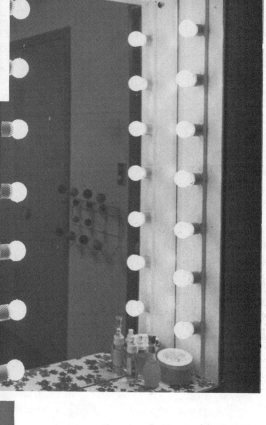

Play-Display Wall

A bit of ingenuity and lighting combine to create this youngster's display-play-cosmetic wall. The top left tackboard is illuminated by 12-volt 25R14 bulbs in painted orange juice cans. The top right shelf is lighted by two F20T12 bulbs with ½-in. eggcrate louvers. Two lower shelves using F15T8 bulbs have diffusing plastic tops. Shelf height is 2½ in. Channels have a convenience outlet. The mirror is lighted with plug-in sockets placed every six inches on the vertical wire mold. Underneath the mirror are the switches and the cord, which plugs into a convenience outlet. Over the bed is a bracket containing two 40-watt fluorescents which provide 25 footcandles for reading.

A 9-inch board conceals three 40-watt deluxe warm-white fluorescent tubes which apply light to the work/play counter of this child's room. Two small, 25-watt reflector floodlights are used to supplement and highlight objects. (Photo courtesy of General Electric)

Table lamps used for reading in bed should again keep the lower edge of the shade at eye level. Recommended shade dimensions: bottom 15-17 inches; top 8-15 inches; depth 10-14 inches. Soft-white 150-200-watt or 50/150-watt bulbs should be used. Placement should be in line with the shoulder and 22 inches to left or right of book center. Extended-arm wall lamps, or fixtures centered two feet from the wall, will span wide headboards to bring light to the desired location. Bulbs should be 100, 150 or 200-watt. Placement is the same as for table lamps.

Fluorescent wall brackets vary in length as follows: single bed, one 36-inch 30-watt deluxe warm-white tube; single bed in corner, an around-the-corner bracket using two 30-watt 36-inch deluxe warm-white tubes; doublebed, one 48-inch 40-watt deluxe warm-white tube; king-size bed or twin beds, two 36-inch or two 48-inch tubes mounted end-to-end as a single unit. Location should be mounted on the wall so the lower edge of the faceboard will be 30 inches above the mattress.

In selecting all types of lighting for children's rooms, keep in mind that fluorescents deliver three times as much light as incandescents for the same wattage, and last 20 times longer. Always select deluxe warm-white or deluxe cool-white for best color effects.

8
Walls & Window Ware

WALL COVERINGS

Color, texture and pattern are the key elements in creating special room settings, whether for children or adults. Your basic knowledge of easily used water-base paints can be applied specifically to the child's room, or you may prefer to advance another step and surface the walls and ceiling with wall coverings.

Wallpapers

Wallpapers are classified as water-sensitive and water-resistant. Water-sensitive wallpapers include roller prints, and screen or hand-printed papers. Roller prints are made by machine with colors applied simultaneously from one, two, or as many as 12 rollers. Prices of roller prints vary depending upon the weight and quality of paper used, the complexity of the design, and the number of yards manufactured.

Screen or hand prints are colored manually by using a separate screen for each color of the design. Since the hand process takes time and skill, these papers are expensive.

Water-resistant wallpapers include part-vinyl or all-vinyl versions that are available as plain acrylic, vinyl, foil, or flock. They are durable, rough, cleanable and last longer than regular wallpaper, and should be a preferred choice for children's rooms.

Wallpaper can be purchased unpasted or prepasted, with the latter type much preferred by homeowner applicators. Prepasted paper has a glue already applied to the back so the material can be simply dipped in water and hung. Often, however, a thin coat of wheat paste is needed, particularly at the edges. Unpasted papers can be applied with several types of paste. It's best to ask the wallpaper dealer for advice related to the specific area where you are to apply the material.

Different wallpapers come in different widths with each single roll covering approximately 30 to 36 square feet regardless of varying widths and lengths. Rolls are usually packaged in 2-roll bolts.

You can estimate your room requirements by measuring the distance in feet around the room, measuring the height of the walls to be covered, and multiplying the two total figures. You can usually deduct one single roll of approximately 30 square feet for each two openings (door) of ordinary size.

Most walls need some preparation before covering them up. Wallpapers will not adhere to dirt, soap and grease. Clean the walls with household soap powder or ammonia, and rinse with clean water. Remove old, loose wallpaper. If it is on tight, sand it down, glue down loose edges, size and paper over it—except for metallics, flocks, foils and embossed patterns, which cannot be papered over.

Grease and dirt should be washed off with a household detergent. Remove any loose or flaking paint and fill in all the cracks with crack filler, then sand to a smooth finish. Most paper manufacturers also recommend application of a coat of wall size, which assures an even surface for the wallpaper to adhere to. Let the size dry before doing anything else.

For new and unpainted walls, use a single coat of pigmented sealer and then coat with size. Glossy painted surfaces should be washed down with detergent, thoroughly sanded, and then covered with a brush coat of wall size before applying wallpaper.

There are numerous "tricks of the trade" in applying wallpaper and most retail dealers will supply you with folders illustrating the steps involved. A few notes worthy of mention, however, are listed below.

- Always hang the ceiling before the walls. It's easier to hang shorter strips (width-wise of the room), but consider the whole room when you decide in which direction to go.

- Never "wrap" a whole strip around inside corners without cutting and re-aligning. It may look okay at first, but in a few weeks, wrinkles and creases might appear.
- When using no-match, plain textured wallpapers, try reversing every other strip top to bottom for more uniform color.
- Never use a seam roller on flocked wallpapers. Gently tap the seams with the edge of the smoothing brush.
- Check the run numbers on your rolls before you start to make sure they're the same, as color may vary slightly from run to run.
- Ceilings, like walls, are not always "true." So plan to end the ceiling wallpaper on the less critical side of the room, like above the entrance.
- When using the same pattern on the ceilings and wall, it can only be matched one way—so choose the direction most prominent to the eye.

Usually, nearly everything you need for applying wallpaper is around the house, including stepladder, yardstick, scissors, pencil, string, chalk, razor knife, a bucket of clean water, and a sponge. You will also need a smoothing brush, seam and paste roller (or a waterbox if hanging prepasted wallpaper).

Paneling

The availability of moderately priced, expensive-looking do-it-yourself paneling has made any decorator's job a great deal easier. In many instances, the addition of one wall of paneling can change the entire appearance of the room.

Paneling over an existing wall is a relatively simple operation with modern materials and accessories. Standard-sized 4 x 8-foot panels are designed to speed installation and minimize necessary cutting and fitting.

Once you have taken delivery, stand the panels separately around the room at least 48 hours prior to installation to acclimate them to room conditions. (Some manufacturers recommend the panels be left flat, separated by blocks to allow air movement, so check this point when making your purchase.)

After pasting smoothly, fold paste to paste so edge ends up just short of center of strip, pattern up. Fold other edge to just beyond the edge of other fold, which should have a few inches without adhesive. Do not crease folds.

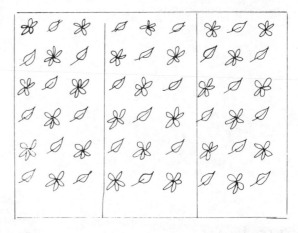

In a drop-match pattern, once you line up the marks, you will find that the first strip has the full pattern at the top. The number two strip will have a half-pattern at the top; the number three strip will also have the full pattern at the top. These three strips illustrate a drop match pattern. Note that every other strip is the same at the top.

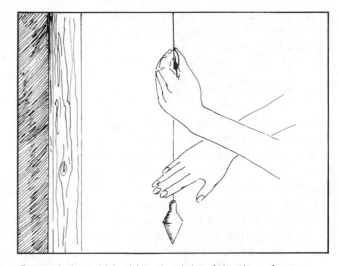

One strip (less ½ inch) to the right of the door, fasten plumb line from ceiling. Chalk the string and, holding it near the bottom, snap a line onto the wall. Measure ceiling height. Allow 3 inches extra top, 3 inches at bottom.

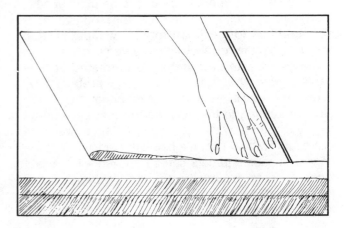

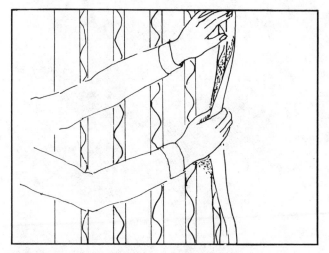

Unfold top part of strip only. Position near ceiling, leaving 3 inches to trim off later. Line up the right edge of the strip with the plumb line.

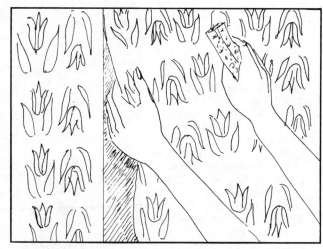

Hang succeeding strips. Carefully match pattern at left edge of new strip with previous strip. Butt edges, sponge, and roll edges.

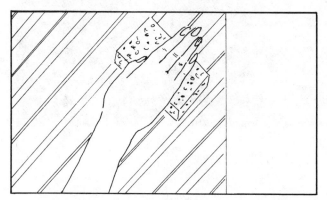

Smooth strip, working from center to edges. Unfold bottom, align with plumb line, smooth out entrapped bubbles with sponge. Small bubbles disappear with drying.

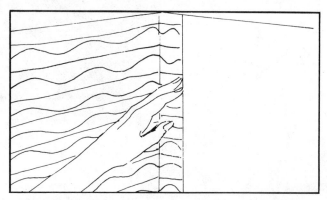

At corner: Measure edge-to-corner at top, middle and baseboard. Take widest measure; add ½ inch. Cut vertical strip this width. Apply, overlap corner ½ inch. Measure next strip. Add ½ inch. Drop plumb this distance from corner. Follow plumb; apply, match pattern and lap at corner.

Use ruler with knife or razor blade to trim top, bottom and around door frame. Wipe off paste with wet sponge. Smooth entire strip. Roll down edges with a seam roller. Don't use roller on flock wall coverings. Tap seams with sponge to avoid matting flock pile.

Windows: Measure ceiling to frame. Add 1 inch. Cut vertical strip, apply so it extends over top of frame 1 inch. Trim around frame. Match pattern; use short lengths above, and below frame.

Built-ins in the child's bedroom can be finished with wallcoverings just as the walls themselves. This Gloria Vanderbilt collection includes a complete alphabet running continuously on different-sized gingham check "building blocks," each 4½" square. Every once in awhile, there's a floral cluster instead, and every letter is filled with tiny flowers, stars, squares as well. (Photo courtesy of James Seeman Studios, Inc.)

Specific installation methods vary with the type of paneling selected and the place of intended use. For example:

- Paneling any existing smooth, flat wall is accomplished using continuous ribbons of adhesive applied at specified intervals over lightly sanded enameled walls, sealed gypsum wallboard or previously wallpapered walls.
- Paneling masonry, cement or other unevenly surfaced walls requires application of 1 x 2, 2 x 3, or 2 x 4-inch furring or framing laid flat against the wall, horizontally on 16-inch centers and vertically on 48-inch centers (masonry must be waterproofed before applying the furring and shims may be required to insure an even surface).

Each panel should be checked for plumb as it is applied to the wall surface. Most manufacturers will recommend you begin the installation in a corner. Use of a scribing compass will enable you to mark corner panels (as well as around windows, doors, etc.) for easy cutting with a coping saw. In making

panel cuts with a power hand-held circular saw, always saw from the back side of the panel using a fine-tooth blade.

Matching color anular threaded nails can be purchased for applying paneling directly to studs or for top and bottom-panel use in combination with adhesives. When adhesives are not used, nail panels every 4 inches along all edges and every 8 inches into intermediate furring.

Solid lumber paneling also can be obtained in various species, patterns and sizes with widths ranging from 6 to 12 inches. This material can be used vertically to make a room seem higher or installed horizontally to make a short room appear longer. Diagonal treatments, random widths and herringbone styles are additional ways of creating unusual effects.

Woodgrain high-pressure decorative plastic laminates are available in vertical grades (as well as the more familiar countertop surfacing grades) for walls. You can also readily obtain simulated brick panels and others resembling stucco finish. Each of these types of paneling may be applied with adhesives.

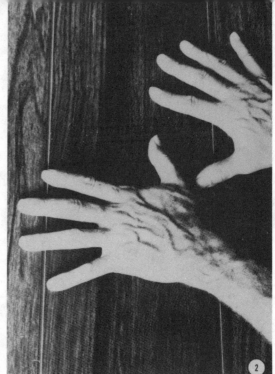

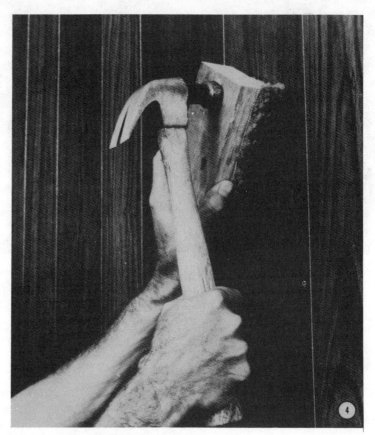

Tips for glue-up application of hardboard panelings: (1) studs or furring strips (in basement application) are first given bead of adhesive and panel is pressed into position carefully so a minimum of shifting is needed after glue contact; (2) apply uniform steady hand pressure to seat in the adhesive; (3) tack-nail with finishing nails at top of sheet leaving heads exposed for later easy removal; (4) use a padded block following a 15-to-20 minute interval to reapply pressure in a final adhesive-setting procedure. Paneling shown is from the Masonite Corporation.

Applying Hardboard Paneling

Big blocky stenciled letters in bright bold colors are the kind of wall decoration that will remain attractive as the child grows. (Penny Lehman designed the room for 1001 Decorating Ideas Magazine.)

Supergraphics

Supergraphics or free designs are growing in popularity for home use as well as the many commercial establishments that use them for a modern decor. These designs can move from wall to wall, floor to ceiling to direct your eye around the room, create headboards, conceal architectural deficiencies and create truly individual living spaces within a given area.

Both paint and wallcoverings are used by

homeowners and interior designers to provide unusual color, texture and pattern. Paint designs can be as expansive as the imagination, ranging from a simple horizontal line ending in an arrow to highly intricate geometrics.

The advent of the poster business in the 1960's brought with it innovations in printing techniques and new approaches in graphic art concepts, which in turn, opened up the possibilities for the first supergraphic wallcoverings. Since that time various firms have entered the marketplace with dozens of

Environmental Graphic's "Moon and Stars" scene is the key focal point of this young adult's bedroom furnished with a modern platform bed and molded plastic seating units. The night time colors are offset by a bright yellow panel at right and the panel doors, one painted deep blue and the other orange.

design statements that have dramatic artistic impact and yet endure as a background for living environments.

Along with the evolution of designs, there has been an accompanying development in lithographic printing ability. The variety of subjects, the quality of work and their reproduction is the result of the combined resources of artist and this advanced lithographic technology.

It's desirable to use washable paint or wallcoverings for supergraphic installations, especially in children's rooms where fingermarks are sure to occur. Wall graphics are sold as complete sets for installation over surfaces smooth-coated with a white sealer. Panels are hung per a schematic provided with each scene, and repeating graphics can be started at any place in the design.

Photomurals

Photomurals have long been popular on office walls, but have now moved into many homes as well.

Inspiring vistas can now be added from floor to ceiling in any room.

Homedecor photomurals produced in Sweden and sold in the United States measure up to 12 feet 8 inches x 9 feet and may be trimmed for smaller walls. Installation requires just a pair of scissors, a brush or two, and the cellulose paste supplied with each lithographed view. Each mural comes precut in easy-to-hang sections. The material is easier to handle than wallpaper and has a varnished surface that can be wiped clean with a wet sponge.

Among the mural wall designs available are these features: Sunset over Lake, Summer Ocean, Wood in Springtime, Autumn Forest, Lake in Mountain, Tropical Sunset, Country Road, Skyline, and others.

Homedecor also markets Photodoors, a series of full-color scenes for slab doors. Again, typical scenes include ocean, sunsets, trees and animals.

Homemade alternative Eastman Kodak, 3M Company and Berkey Photos are among the firms capable of taking your color transparencies (or stock views) and turning them into custom murals mounted on stiff backing for sectional installation in any room. Special lacquers are used to give a custom finish that can be washed. Still other firms and processes make possible the reproduction of full-color transparencies directly onto almost any flexible material, including fabrics, paper and carpeting—but these are fairly expensive.

Posters

Beyond a doubt, the most popular items for decorating teenagers' rooms are wall posters. Where children of the 40's and 50's were satisfied with 8 x 10-inch pinup photos of their favorite athletes or movie stars, today they are in the market for 30 x 40-inch posters of the same.

It's difficult to find a person these days who hasn't seen the Farrah Fawcett-Majors poster first produced in 1976 by Pro Arts, Inc. of Medina, Ohio. Over seven million copies were sold by the time this book was being published. In comparison, the famed swimsuit photo of actress Betty Grable had a printing of three million copies during World War II.

Seeman Studios' complete "Game Time" set of murals includes these four design panels, plus five plain ground, covering a total wall area of 23 in. Each panel is 28 inches wide, with the high point of design 59 inches, and 36 inches of plain ground beneath the design area.

Posters and record album covers are popular wall decorations with the younger set and can be quickly changed as one tires of viewing any scene. This family bath design by Kohler illustrates desirable countertop area, over-the-tub lighting, easy-to-clean floor, and shampoo-style lavatory bowl and fittings.

Pro Arts posters, ranging in size from 8½ by 11-inch to those covering almost 24 square feet, are sold in most every gift shop and discount store in the country. The standard-size poster, 20 x 28-inch, sells for $2.00 (as of January 1979).

Full-color "Signature" action posters of well-known athletes in basketball, tennis, soccer, football, baseball, racquetball, and golf are sold by *Sports Illustrated* for about $3.00 each. The publication also offers a selection of skiing, sailing, and surfing posters in 2 x 3-feet dimensions.

Teenagers by no means are limited to "heroes" for their poster subject matter; less than $10 will bring them their own smiling face, action pose, or scenic.

These posters can be purchased through most camera shops using the purchaser's photo or negative.

WINDOW WARE

Selection of the proper draperies, curtains or other window accessories for a child's room begins with selection of the right hardware for your chosen window treatment.

Window decorating hardware ranges from bold and beautiful decorative rods to the more familiar conventional rods that blend into the background. In making your selection, consider the design of your window, its location, and exactly what you want it to contribute to your room.

Most bedroom windows in older homes are double-hung units, while homes built in recent years tend to have sliding windows. Other children's rooms may have a dormer, bay or casement arrangement.

Interior designers stress a number of questions you should answer before you select any particular type of covering. Included are: Should the window be dramatic or unobtrusive? Will it hide a view or frame a desirable outdoor scene? Will it be opened during the day and closed at night? Need it appear larger or smaller in the total room scheme? Will extra daylight be required for any particular purposes, such as playtime?

While windows are somewhat fixed (not impossible to replace by any means), your decorating treatment can change their shape. Low, squat windows can be made "taller" by using a valance above the window and side draperies. Tier curtains can be used to make windows appear "shorter" or hide trouble spots.

In rooms with northern exposure, it's recommended you use warm colors such as red, orange, yellow and their various color shades such as pink, peach and lemon. Cool colors, like blue, green and violet are restful, and good choices for rooms with a southern exposure. In general, use light colors on large areas and sharp colors as accent.

Window Rods

Here's a rundown on the traditional and decorative rods available, and some of their specific features.

Conventional curtain rods These are threaded through the heading of a sheer curtain that seldom moves, and can project out from the window or fit closely. Close-fitting sash rods can be suspended with hooks or can have rubber ends, or be spring loaded to eliminate the need for screws and nails.

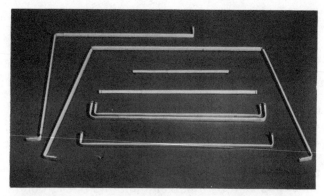

Curtain rods (in top to bottom order) can be purchased to accomplish a special decorating job including: corner window, bay window, sash rod, spring-pressure curtain rod, double curtain rod and single curtain rod. (Photo courtesy of Kirsch Co.)

Cafe rods These rods support curtains or draperies with movable rings. The curtains can be opened or closed by hand or baton. They can be used alone, in two or three tier combination, or with conventional draw draperies.

Conventional traverse rods Adjustable up to 220 inches, they are concealed from view by the heading of the draperies once closed. The "draw" rods can be used separately or in pairs for combining draperies with shirred curtains.

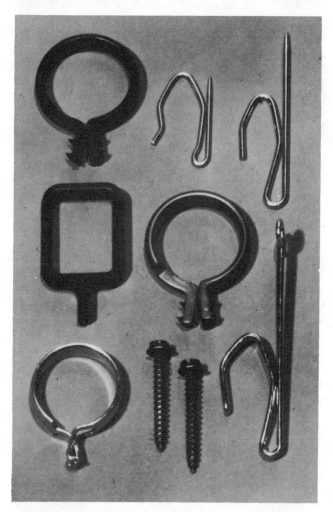

Special hooks, rings and mounting screws can be secured with drapery rods to ensure proper hang and operation. (Photo courtesy of Kirsch Co.)

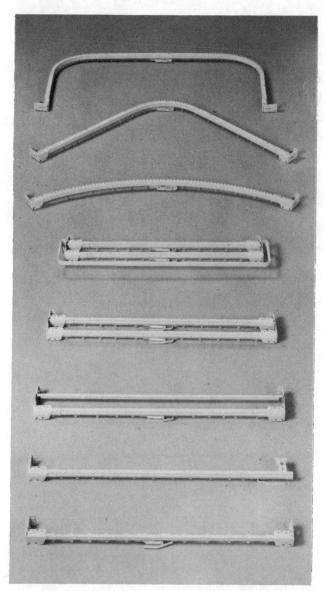

Conventional traverse rods come in a variety of styles, from top to bottom, including: cut-to-measure for rectangular bay, cut-to-measure for corner window, cut-to-measure for bow window, double traverse with valance rod, double traverse, traverse and curtain rod set, one-way-draw traverse and two-way-draw traverse. (Photo courtesy of Kirsch Co.)

Draperies

Today's selection of drapery material is greater than ever. You can choose from numerous textures, patterns, colors and built-in features. It's possible to select satin, openweave, velvet, cotton, linen or almost any other fabric or texture you can think of in unlined or self-lined draperies, or draperies lined with cotton or backed with insulating foam. Major department stores and smaller specialty shops offer draperies in several styles including ready-made, precision, made-to-measure and fully custom-made. You might also consider making your own.

Ready-made draperies generally are pleated to 75 percent of fullness (1½ times) and come in various dimensions "off the rack". Precision-made draperies are ordered in standard widths hemmed to within an inch of the length you specify. Made-to-measure draperies differ from fully custom-made in that you take the measurements to the store for the former, and a drapery expert does the measuring for the latter.

A multi-tier cafe arrangement was used in this boy's room to stretch a small window. Bright blue slats hide the seams of the car-print fabric glued to the adjoining wall areas. (Photo courtesy of Kirsch Co.)

CHART FOR DETERMINING STACKING AREA

Stacking Area Chart. *The stacking area is the space taken up by the draperies when fully open. For a complete view of your window, plan to have the stacking area against the wall on either side of the window glass. Use this chart to determine stacking area for standard glass sizes.*

To determine stacking area for odd-sized windows, measure glass width, divide by three and add 12 inches. This measurement is your stacking area. Then add the stacking area to the glass measurement to get your rod measurement. Make sure this measurement is within the measurement printed on the box. Divide your stacking area by two. Place brackets this distance on either side of glass.

If your draperies are one-way draw, extend rod the full stacking area on one side only. For bulky fabric add 4" to 10" to the stacking area measurement.

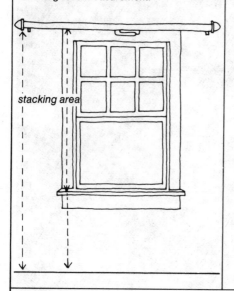

stacking area

If glass is	Stacking area is	Rod must measure	Place bracket this distance on either side of glass
36"	24"	60"	12"
48"	28"	76"	14"
60"	32"	92"	16"
72"	36"	108"	18"
84"	40"	124"	20"
96"	44"	140"	22"
108"	48"	156"	24"
120"	52"	172"	26"
132"	56"	188"	28"
144"	60"	204"	30"
156"	64"	220"	32"
168"	68"	236"	34"
180"	72"	252"	36"
192"	76"	268"	38"
204"	80"	284"	40"
216"	84"	300"	42"

Tips for easier drapery hardware installation.

1. *Avoid miter joint if mounting on casing. Place screws above or below joint.*

2. *If mounting on hollow wall, use special fastening devices such as Molly screw anchors, plastic screw anchors or toggle bolts. Use 1¼" wood screws if you can locate wood studs.*

3. *If using one support, place at center of rod. If using two or more supports, space somewhat equally across the rod but nearer the brackets to support weight of stacked draperies. In some instances, supports are specifically used for inside or outside rod. Check instructions on support envelope.*

4. *Length of adjustable or cut-to-measure conventional traverse or curtain rods is space between brackets, including brackets.*

5. *Length of adjustable decorative cafe and decorative traverse rods does not include finial measurement. If near a corner wall, be sure finial will fit. Rings are not included with decorative cafe rods.*

6. *Cord tension pulleys are recommended for use with longer length traverse rods to keep cords taut and off the floor and to eliminate tangled cords.*

7. *Most conventional traverse rods are adaptable to ceiling installation. Instruction sheets for mounting these rods on the ceiling are packaged with them.*

(Drawings courtesy Kenney Mfg. Company)

Tools to do it Yourself

Tools needed. *Your tools will be a yardstick or steel tape measure (cloth tape stretches) a sharp pair of shears, needles and pins, a thimble, a strong thread in the proper color, and iron and pressing board, and, if you have one, a sewing machine (not necessary but helps you work faster).*

A large working space, such as a broad table, or a clean floor is also essential.

Other things you'll need for top results are good materials, accurate measurements and careful aligning of patterns. And, of course, patience, concentration and care.

Cutting first width. *Before you do anything, cut selvages away or "pink" and clip them so the seams won't pucker and the draperies will hang straight.*

For ease in working with material and to guard against costly mistakes, lay your fabric on a large flat surface when cutting. To insure correct cuts and proper hanging, begin with a true crosswise grain. Don't tear across fabric. In sheer fabrics, pull a thread to see the grain, then cut along its line. In patterned fabric cut evenly across the pattern.

Make the length of your cut the same as you figured when determining the amount of fabric you would need (length wanted plus hem and top and pattern repeat).

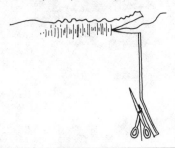

Cutting other widths. *Once you've cut your first width, lay it on top of the fabric remaining to be cut so the pattern matches. Pin all around then cut your second width. Repeat until you have all the widths you need. Remember, not only must each panel and each side of a pair of curtains match, but every window in the room should match according to pattern. Cut enough fabric to make one panel to see how you are doing.*

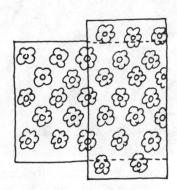

Joining widths into panels. *To avoid a raw edge when joining widths into panels, use a narrow French seam or overcast both edges of seams.*

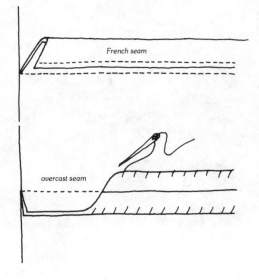

French seam

overcast seam

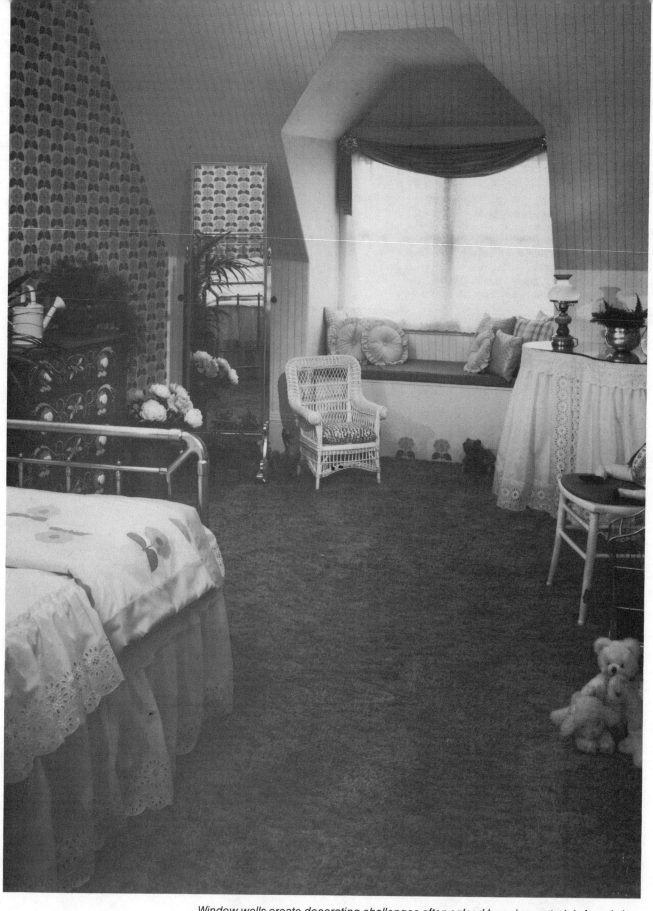

Window wells create decorating challenges often solved by using materials found else-where in the room. This young lady's attic bedroom utilizes an embroidery pattern for bed skirt, table surround and curtains. A swag valence unites the windows, picking up color of the avocado carpeting. Photo: Burlington House Carpets.

Curtains usually are made of sheer or semi-sheer fabrics in shorter lengths than draperies. Only tailored curtain panels and priscilla curtains are more than 45 inches long. Priscilla curtains are very much at home with traditional decor. They're sheer or semi-opaque, and come in widths up to 300 inches per pair. To criss-cross them, multiply the area to be covered by four to arrive at the correct size. (See accompanying stacking-area chart for draperies.) Widths are limited and the curtains usually come in just one width, with flat unpleated top.

Colorful novelty curtains are very popular for children's rooms, and almost all are made of no-iron easy-care fibers. A lot of these curtains have many components available for creating your own effects.

Panels are almost always sheer polyester. White and ecru are traditional favorites but other colors are now available. Some panels have intricate designs and embroidery.

Woven Wood Shades

Another type of window treatment that is rapidly growing in popularity is the woven wood shade which comes in a myriad of colors. These units roll like their fabric relatives or double fold from either top or bottom. Some can even be used as draw draperies or used as cafe curtains or folding doors.

Outside mounting of woven wood shades usually allows a three-inch greater surrounding dimension than the window itself for prevention of a light gap. Inside or recessed mounting is done within the window frame, usually with a valence hiding the mounting elements.

Tight loop carpeting with nylon pile yarns has a built-in soil-hiding property, important to rooms used by teens. This room designed by Pedro Rodrigues, ASID, also employs carpeting for the sleep platforms. The study corner has plenty of light and wall-hung storage. (Photo courtesy of Burlington House Carpets)

9
Stylish & Sturdy Floors

In both new and existing rooms for children you are almost certain to encounter three or perhaps four basic types of materials used in floor construction—hardwood flooring, resilient materials, carpeting and ceramic tile. Each has its own unique features, plus a few drawbacks that may be worth considering if a change is desired.

HARDWOOD

As builders sought ways to cut costs, many newer homes were constructed without hardwood finish flooring. In these homes, the plywood underlayment was installed with the option of either resilient finish flooring or carpeting. In older homes, however, many a carpeted room hides an attractive hardwood surface that often can be put to use with a few hours of sanding and simple refinishing.

Most home hardwood floors are either oak or maple, both long-lasting species put down in long strips or squares. Some types include decorative pegs or parquet geometric patterns such as squares, rectangles, herringbone and basketweave. In purchasing new hardwood flooring, you have the choice of unfinished or slightly more costly prefinished material which speeds installation use of the completed surface.

In refinishing hardwood flooring it's best to rent an electric sanding machine and use it in combination with a small electric hand sander rather than tackle the job non-mechanically. This will save time and mess in removing old finish and restoring an unmarred surface free of scratches, stains and other marks.

Manufacturers recommend use of No. 4 open coat sandpaper for removing varnish from hardwood flooring; No. 3 closed coat sandpaper is suitable for other finishes. A second "cut" is made with No. 0 sandpaper and the final third "cut" with No. 00 or No. 000 sandpaper.

Hardwood floors of old were really never difficult to care for—but old style finishes were. These floors were varnished or shellacked; as the surface coat became scratched, chipped or worn, it required a tough on-your-knees waxing job. Today you can purchase hardwood flooring that has both finish and wax factory-baked deep into the wood fibers with infra-red heat. Such finishes are almost impossible to wear away. Upkeep is reduced to vacuuming when you vacuum your carpet and waxing when you shampoo your carpet.

E.L. Bruce Co., manufacturer of hardwood flooring, recommends a few simple methods for maintenance that's sure to be a part of hardwood flooring in a child's room. Here are their suggestions:

- Food Spots—wipe them up immediately with a damp cloth (not wet); if the surface spot looks a little dull, rub on a little wax.
- White Spots—usually too much wax is the problem; use fine steel wool dampened with wax or mineral spirits and then wipe dry and rub on a little wax.
- Water Spots—try the white spot remedy; if it doesn't work, try fine sandpaper, wipe with mineral spirits, touch up with matching stain and wax.
- Dark (or dog) Spots—try white or water spot treatment, or apply household bleach to spot and let it stand for about an hour; rinse with a wet cloth, wipe dry, smooth with steel wool or fine sandpaper, touch up with matching stain and wax.
- Ink Stains—try household bleach or oxalic acid from the drug store, or lightly sand, wash with mineral spirits, retouch with stain and then wax.
- Greasy Spots—rub grease, tar or oil with cloth or fine steel wool dampened with mineral spirits; this usually lifts lipstick, crayon and rubber marks, too.

Floor surfaces in rooms designed primarily for children can be a combination of materials. Here sculptured carpeting surrounds a "Race to the Magic Kingdom" nylon carpet which combines the recognition of familiar Walt Disney characters with favorite games of childhood. (Photo courtesy of Jorges Carpet Mills, Inc.)

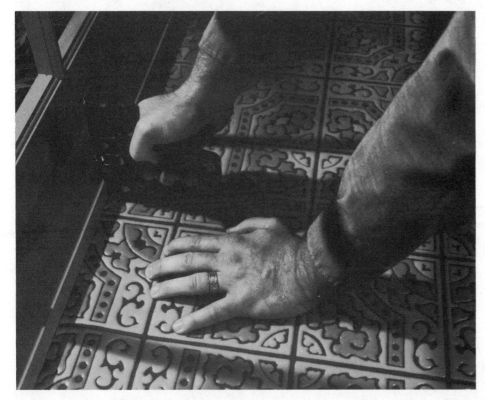

Cushioned vinyl floor that comes folded like a blanket and installs with a staple gun takes much of the previous work out of installing a new floor in a child's room. The do-it-yourselfer can trim to less than perfectly but still obtain a perfect fit—the material can be stretched. The material also can be cemented to concrete surfaces. (Photo courtesy of Armstrong Cork Co.)

RESILIENT SHEET OR TILE

Resilient flooring long has been popular in children's rooms and even more so now with the introduction of the "wet look" vinyl materials that require no waxing. Literally hundreds of colors and patterns are available for bedrooms, play rooms, attics, basements and those places most inhabited by children.

Sheet vinyl flooring now comes in 6, 9 and 12-foot widths to eliminate the need for seams in most rooms. The material often has a built-in cushioned layer, and in some instances can be installed wall-to-wall without adhesive.

The low cost factor of sheet vinyl flooring (and other resilient materials) makes it possible for the budget-minded to more easily decorate for a child's different life cycles. For example, the young couple can select specific "nursery" colors and scenes featuring animals, stuffed toys, etc. and later change to sports and teenage interests at not too high a cost.

CERAMIC TILE

Ceramic tile, once confined primarily to bathroom floors and kitchen countertops, now can be found throughout the home—even in children's rooms. This material is so old that it predates Western history, yet so new that usage reached 502 million square feet in 1977, a 29 percent increase over the previous year.

Much of the reason for the increased popularity of ceramic tile can be attributed to pattern and color. Units that are a larger size than the standard 4¼-inch squares plus the advent of colored tile grout have opened new design avenues in the home. Decorators readily use this material for bedrooms, family rooms and outdoor patio and play areas in addition, of course, to floors, walls and countertops in kitchens and bathrooms.

Ceramic tile is a mixture of clays that are baked at extremely high temperature to make the body harden and the shape permanent. When the color is sprayed on before the mixture goes into the kiln for firing, it's called glazed tile. When the color goes all the way through the body, it's either quarry tile (which comes in natural clay colors) or ceramic mosaics (clay mixed with natural pigment). No matter what the color, the tile from the kiln is permanent, beautiful, waterproof and simple to clean.

Many homeowners prefer to leave tile setting to the professionals, but this material is certainly no mystery for the handy do-it-yourselfer. A complete set of tile installation tools can be rented from your

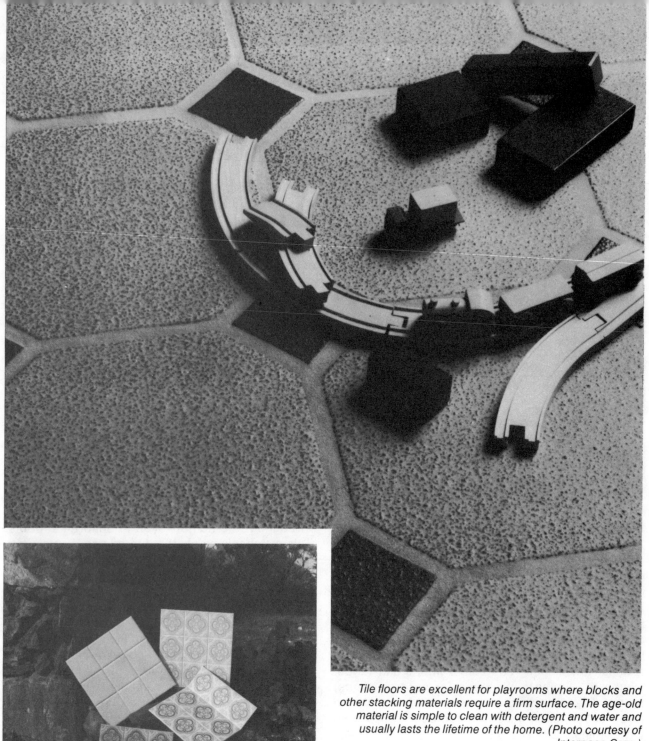

Tile floors are excellent for playrooms where blocks and other stacking materials require a firm surface. The age-old material is simple to clean with detergent and water and usually lasts the lifetime of the home. (Photo courtesy of Interpace Corp.)

Easy-Set ceramic tile sheets make it possible for the home-owner to include colorful ceramic tile in children's rooms, applying the material to any flat, clean, sound surface with an adhesive. The sheets are factory grouted with silicone rubber. Of the patterns shown here, the top four are for walls and the lower four for floors. (Photo courtesy of American Olean Tile Co.)

tile dealer for a few dollars and he'll be glad to provide you with detailed written instructions for accomplishing your specific task.

You can install ceramic tile over most any structurally sound, dry, clean and level surface such as double-wood flooring, ½-inch exterior type plywood, ceramic tile, steel-troweled cement, asphalt or vinyl tile or sheet flooring. Loose and damaged plaster, wallpaper and paint should be removed before tiling. Grease should be removed, newly plastered walls sealed, and glossy or painted surfaces sanded.

CARPETING

Carpet experts suggest a one-two-three method of selecting carpet and rugs for children's rooms as well as all other spaces in the home—first, decide on the color; next, choose the texture; and then choose fiber by performance desired.

Carpet color can be one of the most versatile elements in room decorating and opens countless possibilities suggested by a quick glance at the familiar color wheel. Warm colors—yellow, orange, red and the others—can make a room seem smaller, or make a sunless room cozier. The cool colors —greens, blues, lilacs—make a room seem larger and more spacious, and can cool down a too-sunny exposure.

Interior designers will urge you to select your floor color first and then coordinate the rest of your draperies, walls, furniture, and accessories with it.

Carpet Properties

The Carpet and Rug Institute reports that wool remains a traditional leader in higher-priced and luxury lines. It resists soil and is easy to clean. It's warm, resilient, soft and comfortable.

Nylon carpet wears exceptionally well, dyes easily and is colorfast, resists soil and is easy to clean. Acrylic looks and feels like wool, is lightweight, has fluffy pile and cleans well. Polyester is a soft, but durable, fiber that makes excellent shag carpeting. It has low-static tendencies and is high in ease-of-care characteristics. Olefin, excellent for children's baths, kitchens, laundries and outdoor use, has great strength and resists stain and soil. Colors are bright, clear and sharp, and static build-up is low.

Sound Control

Teenagers and their love of loud sounds (sometimes called music) have done much to enhance the application of carpeting not only to floors but also walls and even ceilings.

It's a well accepted fact that walking on a carpeted floor produces less noise than any other type of flooring. Further acoustical laboratory studies have shown that carpet and rugs help absorb three types of noise: airborne, floor surface and impact. The voice carries, echoes and produces a very loud sound in an empty room—this is airborne noise. The sound of metal nails in the heels of shoes on tile floors can be distracting—this is floor surface noise. The thud of something hitting a wooden floor is a common sound—this is impact noise.

Quantity Needed

One of the first questions which will have to be answered when shopping for a new carpet is the size of the area to be covered. It's a good idea to have a rough sketch with measurements of the area to be carpeted before visiting your local carpet retailer. This sketch can be made on plain paper, but graph paper ruled in small squares is even easier to use.

A long measuring tape should be used to obtain room dimensions. If a yardstick is used, it is a good idea to remeasure the area to avoid errors. All measurements should be in feet, and all inches less than one foot should be dropped and the total number of feet increased by one. For example, 21 feet and 10½ inches should be changed to 22 feet.

Multiplying the total number of feet in one direction by the feet in the other will give the total number of square feet. If the total number of square feet is divided by 9, this will give the minimum number of square yards needed to cover the area. It is quite likely the amount of carpeting needed will be slightly larger than this minimum amount.

Most carpet is made 12 feet wide, but some is produced in other widths. If the room measures 11 feet by 14 feet then the minimum square yards would be a little over 17 (11 feet x 14 feet = 154 square feet; 154 square feet divided by 9 feet = square yards). However, in order to install this minimum amount, seaming of small pieces at one end would be necessary. This would probably not only be more costly due to additional cost of installation, but the many seams would look unsightly. Therefore, the amount of carpet normally used would be 18²/₃ square yards (12 feet x 14 feet divided by 9) so one piece of carpet, without seams, could be installed. Even though it may be a little more costly for the carpet, the end result would be well worth it. This is the reason for a sketch as well as dimensions when buying carpet. If the carpet has a pattern and seams have to be made, additional carpet will be needed. The extra carpet is needed to match the pattern.

In figuring the amount of carpeting you'll need for a child's room (or any other room) you should take into consideration bay windows, closets, doorways and other odd areas. These areas may be small and the amount of carpet needed to cover them may seem insignificant, but if they are not taken into consideration they may end up not covered, or it may result in poor placement of a seam.

If a room is wider than the width of the carpet, then it will require a seam. A sketch is helpful in planning the best place to locate this seam.

A sketch is also helpful if an area rug or room size rug is to be purchased. The size of the rug can be drawn on the sketch. This will show the area that it will cover or what is needed to be covered.

10
Safety

FIRE PROTECTION

Smoke Detectors

No children's room improvement should be completed without the addition of a nearby smoke detector. The device should generally be installed on the ceiling leading to bedrooms, and away from kitch-

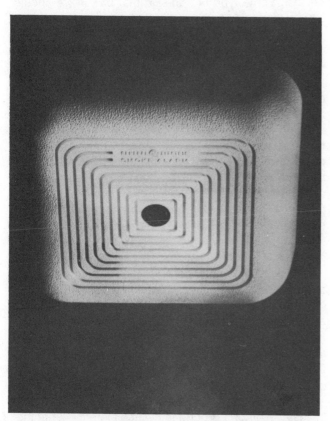

This smoke alarm is able to detect the presence of combustion particles and sound a loud alarm when smoke reaches it. Pushing the center button permits the homeowner to check from time to time to see the battery-operated unit is energized and working. (Photo of "Home Sentry" Alarm, courtesy of General Electric)

ens and fireplaces where they can be touched off accidentally. In two-story dwellings, there should be two alarms, one on the first floor and one upstairs.

The reasoning behind use of smoke detectors is easily understood when one is confronted with this figure: 6000 annual residential fire deaths occur in the United States each year, most of them even before the flames have broken out. Fire department films show that smoke and toxic gasses float above the bed of a sleeping child (or adult). When the sleeper wakes and sits up, one breath of the poisonous fumes can kill. And that's even before there's any danger from flames or heat.

Smoke detectors react before there is visible smoke (and before it could surround the child's bed) because they measure combustion particles in the air. This is important, since the least diminishment of oxygen in the air affects the brain. Usually there is 20 percent oxygen in the brain; if it drops to just 17 percent, judgment is affected—resulting in panic and death.

There are dozens of smoke detectors on the market and their popularity can be measured by an increase in sales from 12 million sold in 1977 to 16.5 million in 1978. All of the units are either ionization detectors which operate on batteries, or photoelectric devices that usually plug into a wall outlet. This latter type also may be wired into the home electrical system.

It is important to you to select a model that cannot be accidentally turned off by a light switch or unplugged by a child. It is also important to regularly check any battery to be certain it has not gone dead. Some of the detectors have devices that tell you if the batteries are in place and working.

Smoke detectors are round, light-colored plastic domes that emit piercing siren-like wails at the first hint of smoke in the home. Cigarette smoke can cause a false alarm (or be used to test the unit). Prices of smoke alarms have been dropping substantially since their introduction several years ago. Today, you can purchase UL-approved devices for under $25.

Portable Ladders

Portable fire escapes are available from a number of manufacturers; the best feature all-steel construction and provide good support and fire resistance. Fire escape ladders are usually made of heavy steel link, with steel rungs that are placed about 18 inches apart. Two hooks hang over the window sill and help keep the ladder away from the burning building. The hooks fold for easy storage of the ladder under a bed, or on the floor of a closet.

POISONINGS

Tens of thousands are killed or seriously injured each year in home accidents, many of these persons being youngsters. One potentially dangerous place in the house is the bathroom, because that is where the medicine cabinet is located. Even though the bathroom ranks far down the list of lethal rooms, it particularly causes trouble for children under four years of age. Several hundred children die each year from poisoning of some sort or other.

The U.S. Public Health Service lists these items as the principal killers of young children: aspirin, bleach, insecticides, soaps and detergents, and vitamins and iron preparations. Be sure that all bottles are accurately labelled and placed out of the child's reach.

Electrical Hazards

Electrical shocks are another child (as well as adult) hazard, especially in the bathroom where a person taking a bath makes contact with a plug-in radio, hair drier or other appliance connected to an outlet. Outlets should be as far away from water and pipes as possible, and no electrical appliance should be used while bathing. Carpeting, rather than bare floor, also helps prevent electrical shock.

Extension cords are a common hazard to young children, who put the cords into mouths and receive burns. These wires should never be installed under carpet and, if you must use them in a child-accessible place, cover unused outlets with electrical tape to prevent accidental insertion of shock-producing objects. Floor-level and child-accessible unused wall outlets should be safeguarded by inserting plastic plugs, available at your local hardware store.

SAFETY IN THE BATHROOM

The bathroom is such a familiar area of the house that we all tend to forget it can also be one of the most dangerous. Here, within a relatively small space, the hazards of water and electricity can combine to cause injury and even death.

Consumer activist Ralph Nader reports that nearly 900 Americans die every year as a result of injuries suffered in bathrooms, and another 187,000 are hurt seriously enough to require hospitalization or emergency room treatment. Falls, burns, cuts, electrocutions—all are possible.

The National Safety Council warns that "tile floors are a real threat when wet. Keep them wiped dry and use a non-skid mat on the floor, especially near the tub or shower where there is likely to be water on the floor."

Manufacturers are now producing bathtubs with permanent non-slip surfaces, but bathroom fixtures last for many years so that millions of homes have only the old type of tub with slippery porcelain enamel underfoot. Some type of non-skid mat or surface should be provided, along with sturdy grab bars.

Burns can occur in a bathroom probably more frequently than in any other area of a home, except around the kitchen range. The hazards of gushing hot water to infants and small children are notorious as a cause of death and disfigurement. But even adults can suffer, especially where a too-narrow shower pipe can cause a sudden rush of hot water when cold water is turned on elsewhere in the house. There are simple means to avoid this hazard. The National Safety Council recommends mixer faucets on the washbowl and a mixer valve or faucet in the shower. The most practical immediate step is simply to make sure the thermostat on the hot water heater is kept at a safe level. Water heated to 115° Fahrenheit or above is destructive to human tissue.

Electricity in combination with the water sources in a bathroom probably is the greatest hazard of all. Lighting fixtures, electrical outlets, and wall switches, all are grouped around washbowls, tubs, and showers. Family members using this room frequently have damp hands, damp bodies, or are standing on damp floors. Any malfunction in an electrical appliance can be disastrous.

The danger of shock could be completely eliminated by installation of a ground fault circuit interrupter at the fuse box of the house. These are now required in most building codes for outdoor electrical receptacles, and would be a great factor in improving home safety if they were considered equally important inside a house.

Some of the other common bathroom hazards are

pinpointed in this simple home safety quiz for the bathroom provided by the National Safety Council:

Do you:

- Have non-skid mats or textured surfaces in tubs and showers?
- Have a sturdy grab bar for your tub or shower?
- Have medicines clearly labeled and read the label before taking any medicine?
- Keep medicines stored safely out of the reach of small children?
- Dry your hands before using electrical appliances—and never operate them when you're in the bathtub.

Injuries

Each year the National Injury Identification Clearinghouse releases a "danger index" based on the number of injuries reported to hospital emergency rooms and the severity of injuries. In the most recent report 12 of the top 13 "hazards" are specifically related to children. In order the top 13 are:

- Bicycles and related equipment
- Stairs, steps, ramps and landings
- Football activity and equipment
- Baseball activity and equipment
- Swings, slides, seesaws and playground equipment
- Power lawnmowers
- Skates, skateboards and scooters
- Swimming and swimming pools
- Non-glass tables
- Beds, springs, and bed frames
- Chairs, sofas and sofa beds
- Basketball activity and equipment
- Floors and flooring

Accidents also occur due to slippery floors in the bathroom. Traditionally, people have used resilient flooring or ceramic tile for floor covering in the bathroom. Currently, housing specialists recommend everything except wood strip or wood block flooring for this room, even when it is to be used primarily by children. Particularly recommended is foam-back carpeting; it is soft underfoot, prevents slipping, and can be easily removed for cleaning.

Manufacturers' List

American Olean Tile Co., Lansdale, PA 19446
American Plywood Assn., 1119 A St., Tacoma, WA 98401
American-Standard, Box 2003, New Brunswick, NJ 08903
Armstrong Cork Co., Lancaster, PA 17604

Bassett Furniture Industries, Inc., Box 626, Bassett, VA 24055
Berkey K&L Laboratory, 222 E. 44th St., N.Y., NY 10017
Bilco Co., 37 Water St., New Haven, CO 06505
Burlington Industries, Inc., Valley Forge Corporate Center, King of Prussia, PA 19406

California Redwood Assn., 617 Montgomery St., San Francisco, CA 94111
Carpet & Rug Institute, Box 2048, Dalton, GA 30720
Closet Maid Corp., 720 SW 17th St., Ocala, FL 32670

Eastman Kodak Co., 343 State St., Rochester, NY 14608
Eljer Plumbingware, 3 Gateway Center, Pittsburgh, PA 15222
Ethan Allen, Inc., Ethan Allen Dr., Danbury, CO 06810

Fieldcrest, 60 W. 40th St., N.Y., NY 10018
Formica Corp., Formica Building, 120 E. 4th St., Cincinnati, OH 45202

GAF Corp., 140 W. 51st St., N.Y., NY 10020
General Electric Co., Wiring Div., Bridgeport, CO 06602
General Electric Co., Lamp Div., Nela Park, Cleveland, OH 44112

Haas Cabinet Co., 613 W. Utica St., Sellersburg, IN 47172
Homedecor, Div. of Baron Organization, Inc., 2355 Salzedo St., Coral Gables, FL 33134
House of Hammocks, Box 613, Falmouth, MA 02541
H.U.D.D.L.E., 3416 Wesley St., Culver City, CA 90230

Imperial Wallcoverings, Collins & Aikman, 210 Madison Ave., N.Y., NY 10016
Interpace Corp., 2901 Los Feliz Blvd., Los Angeles, CA 90039

Jorges Carpet Mills, Inc., Box 698, Rossville, GA 30741

Kenny Mfg. Co., Warwick, RI 02887
Kirsch Co., 309 Prospect St., Sturgis, MI 49091
Kohler Co., Kohler, WI 53044
Koppers Co., Inc., Pittsburgh, PA 15219

Lightcraft of California, NuTone Div., 1600 W. Slauson Ave., Los Angeles, CA 90047

Masonite Corp., 29 N. Wacker Dr., Chicago, IL 60606

National Oak Floor Mfgs. Assn., 814 Sterick Building, Memphis, TN 38103
National Woodwork Manufacturers Assn., 355 Lexington Ave., N.Y., NY 10017
Nils Anderson Studios, Inc., Bear Creek Rd., Johnsonburg, NJ 07846

Ondine, Div. of Interbath, Inc., 427 N. Baldwin Park Blvd., City of Industry, CA 91746
Ozite, A Brunswick Co., 1755 Butterfield Rd., Libertyville, IL 60048

Pasha Pillow Co., 1398 Main St., San Francisco, CA 94124
Pro-Arts, Medina, OH

Seeman Studios, Inc., 50 Rose Place, Garden City, LI, NY 11040
Syroco Furniture, Syracuse, NY 13201

3M Company, 3M Center, St. Paul, MN 55101

Time, Inc., Rockefeller Center, N.Y., NY 10020

Wallcovering Industry Bureau, 1099 Wall St. West, Lyndhurst, NJ 07071
Wessel Hardware Corp., Erie Ave. & D St., Philadelphia, PA 19134
Western Wood Products Assn., 1500 Yeon Building, Portland, OR 97204
Window Shade Manufacturers Assn., 230 Park Ave., N.Y., NY 10017

Z-Brick Co., Div. of VMC, 2834 NW Market St., Seattle, WA 98107

Index

Other SUCCESSFUL Books

SUCCESSFUL PLANTERS, Orcutt. "Definitive book on container gardening." *Philadelphia Inquirer.* Build a planter, and use it for a room divider, a living wall, a kitchen herb garden, a centerpiece, a table, an aquarium—and don't settle for anything that looks homemade! Along with construction steps, there is advice on the best types of planters for individual plants, how to locate them for best sun and shade, and how to provide the best care to keep plants healthy and beautiful, inside or outside the home. 8½"x11"; 136 pp; over 200 photos and illustrations. Cloth $12.00. Paper $4.95.

BOOK OF SUCCESSFUL FIREPLACES, 20th ed., Lytle. The expanded, updated edition of the book that has been a standard of the trade for over 50 years—over a million copies sold! Advice is given on selecting from the many types of fireplaces available, on planning and adding fireplaces, on building fires, on constructing and using barbecues. Also includes new material on wood as a fuel, woodburning stoves, and energy savings. 8½"x11"; 128 pp; over 250 photos and illustrations. $5.95 Paper.

SUCCESSFUL ROOFING & SIDING, Reschke. "This well-illustrated and well-organized book offers many practical ideas for improving a home's exterior." *Library Journal.* Here is full information about dealing with contractors, plus instructions specific enough for the do-it-yourselfer. All topics, from carrying out a structural checkup to supplemental exterior work like dormers, insulation, and gutters, fully covered. Materials to suit all budgets and home styles are reviewed and evaluated. 8½"x11"; 160 pp; over 300 photos and illustrations. $5.95 Paper. (Main selection Popular Science and McGraw-Hill Book Clubs)

PRACTICAL & DECORATIVE CONCRETE, Wilde. "Spells it all out for you...is good for beginner or talented amateur..." *Detroit Sunday News.* Complete information for the layman on the use of concrete inside or outside the home. The author—Executive Director of the American Concrete Institute—gives instructions for the installation, maintenance, and repair of foundations, walkways, driveways, steps, embankments, fences, tree wells, patios, and also suggests "fun" projects. 8½"x11"; 144 pp; over 150 photos and illustrations. $12.00 Cloth.

SUCCESSFUL HOME ADDITIONS, Schram. For homeowners who want more room but would like to avoid the inconvenience and distress of moving, three types of home additions are discussed: garage conversion with carport added; bedroom, bathroom, sauna addition; major home renovation which includes the addition of a second-story master suite and family room. All these remodeling projects have been successfully completed and, from them, step-by-step coverage has been reported of almost all potential operations in adding on to a home. The straightforward presentation of information on materials, methods, and costs, as well as a glossary of terms, enables the homeowner to plan, arrange contracting, or take on some of the work personally in order to cut expenses. 8½"x11"; 144 pp; over 300 photos and illustrations. Cloth $12.00. Paper $5.95.

FINISHING OFF, Galvin. A book for both the new-home owner buying a "bonus space" house, and those who want to make use of previously unused areas of their homes. The author advises which jobs can be handled by the homeowner, and which should be contracted out. Projects include: putting in partitions and doors to create rooms; finishing off floors and walls and ceilings; converting attics and basements; designing kitchens and bathrooms, and installing fixtures and cabinets. Information is given for materials that best suit each job, with specifics on tools, costs, and building procedures. 8½"x11"; 144 pp; over 250 photos and illustrations. Cloth $12.00. Paper $5.95.

SUCCESSFUL FAMILY AND RECREATION ROOMS, Cornell. How to best use already finished rooms or convert spaces such as garage, basement, or attic into family/recreation rooms. Along with basics like lighting, ventilation, plumbing, and traffic patterns, the author discusses "mood setters" (color schemes, fireplaces, bars, etc.) and finishing details (flooring, wall covering, ceilings, built-ins, etc.) A special chapter gives quick ideas for problem areas. 8½"x11"; 144 pp; over 250 photos and diagrams. (Featured alternate for McGraw-Hill Book Clubs.) $12.00 Cloth. $4.95 Paper.

SUCCESSFUL HOME GREENHOUSES, Scheller. Instructions, complete with diagrams, for building all types of greenhouses. Among topics covered are: site location, climate control, drainage, ventilation, use of sun, auxiliary equipment, and maintenance. Charts provide characteristics and requirements of plants and greenhouse layouts are included in appendices. "One of the most completely detailed volumes of advice for those contemplating an investment in a greenhouse." *Publishers Weekly.* 8½"x11"; 136 pp; over 200 photos and diagrams. (Featured alternates of the Popular Science and McGraw-Hill Book Clubs). $12.00 Cloth. $4.95 Paper.

SUCCESSFUL SPACE SAVING AT HOME, Galvin. The conquest of inner space in apartments, whether tiny or ample, and homes, inside and out. Storage and built-in possibilities for all living areas, with a special section of illustrated tips from the professional space planners. 8½"x11"; 128 pp; over 150 B-W and color photographs and illustrations. $12.00 Cloth. $4.95 Paper.

SUCCESSFUL KITCHENS, 2nd ed., Galvin. Updated and revised edition of the book *Workbench* called "A thorough and thoroughly reliable guide to all phases of kitchen design and construction. Special features include how to draw up your own floor plan and cabinet arrangement, plus projects such as installing countertops, dishwashers, cabinets, flooring, lighting, and more. 8½"x11"; 144 pp; over 250 photos and illustrations, incl. color. Cloth $12.00. Paper $5.95.

SUCCESSFUL LIVING ROOMS, Hedden. A collection of projects to beautify and add enjoyment to living and dining areas. The homeowner will be able to build a bar, dramatize lighting, enhance or brighten up an old fireplace, build entertainment centers, and make structural changes. "The suggestions…are imaginative. A generous number of illustrations make the book easy to understand. Directions are concisely written…new ideas, superior presentation." *Library Journal.* 8½"x11"; 152 pp; over 200 illustrations and photos, incl. color. Cloth $12.00. Paper $5.95.

SUCCESSFUL LANDSCAPING, Felice. Tips and techniques on planning and caring for lawns, trees, shrubs, flower and vegetable gardens, and planting areas. "Profusely illustrated…this book can help those looking for advice on improving their home grounds. Thorough details." *Publishers Weekly.* "Comprehensive handbook." *American Institute of Landscape Architects.* Also covers building fences, decks, bird baths and feeders, plus climate-and-planting schedules, and a glossary of terms and chemical products. 8½"x11"; 128 pp; over 200 illustrations including color; $12.00 Cloth. $4.95 Paper.

IMPROVING THE OUTSIDE OF YOUR HOME, Schram. This complete guide to an attractive home exterior at low cost covers every element, from curb to chimney to rear fence. Emphasis is on house facade and attachments, with tips on enhancing natural settings and adding manmade features. Basic information on advantages or disadvantages of materials plus expert instructions make it easy to carry out repairs and improvements that increase the home's value and reduce its maintenance. 8½"x11"; 168 pp; over 250 illustrations including color; $12.00 Cloth. $5.95 Paper.

SUCCESSFUL LOG HOMES, Ritchie. Log homes are becoming increasingly popular—low cost, ease of construction and individuality being their main attractions. This manual tells how to work from scratch whether cutting or buying logs—or how to remodel an existing log structure—or how to build from a prepackaged kit. The author advises on best buys, site selection, evaluation of existing homes, and gives thorough instructions for building and repair. 8½"x11"; 168 pp; more than 200 illustrations including color. $12.00 Cloth. $5.95 Paper.

SUCCESSFUL SMALL FARMS—BUILDING PLANS & METHODS, Leavy. A comprehensive guide that enables the owner of a small farm to plan, construct, add to, or repair buildings at least expense and without disturbing his production. Emphasis is on projects the farmer can handle without a contractor, although advice is given on when and how to hire work out. Includes basics of farmstead layout, livestock housing, environmental controls, storage needs, fencing, building construction and preservation, and special needs. 8½"x11"; 192 pp; over 250 illustrations. $14.00 Cloth. $5.95 Paper.

SUCCESSFUL HOME REPAIR—WHEN *NOT* TO CALL THE CONTRACTOR. Anyone can cope with household repairs or emergencies using this detailed, clearly written book. The author offers tricks of the trade, recommendations on dealing with repair crises, and step-by-step repair instructions, as well as how to set up a preventive maintenance program. 8½"x11"; 144 pp; over 150 illustrations. $12.00 Cloth. $4.95 Paper.

OUTDOOR RECREATION PROJECTS, Bright. Transform you backyard into a relaxation or game area—without enormous expense—using the instructions in this book. There are small-scale projects such as putting greens, hot tubs, or children's play areas, plus more ambitious ventures including tennis courts and skating rinks. Regional differences are considered; recommendations on materials, construction methods are given as are estimated costs. "Will encourage you to build the patio you've always wanted, install a tennis court or boat dock, or construct playground equipment…Bright provides information on choosing tools, selecting lumber, and paving with concrete, brick or stone." *House Beautiful.* (Featured alternate Popular Science and McGraw-Hill Book Clubs). 8½"x11"; 160 pp; over 200 photos and illustrations including color. $12.00 Cloth. $5.95 Paper.

SUCCESSFUL WOOD BOOK—HOW TO CHOOSE, USE, AND FINISH EVERY TYPE OF WOOD, Bard. Here is the primer on wood—how to select it and use it effectively, efficiently, and safely—for all who want to panel a wall, build a house frame, make furniture, refinish a floor, or carry out any other project involving wood inside or outside the home. The author introduces the reader to wood varieties and their properties, describes major wood uses, advises on equipping a home shop, and covers techniques for working with wood including the use of paints and stains. 8½"x11"; 160 pp; over 250 illustrations including color. $12.00 Cloth. $5.95 Paper.

SUCCESSFUL PET HOMES, Mueller. "There are years worth of projects…The text is good and concise—all around, I am most impressed." *Roger Caras, Pets and Wildlife, CBS.* "A thoroughly delightful and helpful book for everyone who loves animals." *Syndicated reviewer, Lisa Oglesby.* Here is a new approach to keeping both pet owners and pets happy by choosing, buying, building functional but inexpensive houses, carriers, feeders, and play structures for dogs, cats, and birds. The concerned pet owner will find useful advice on providing for pet needs with the least wear and tear on the home. 8½"x11"; 116 pp; over 200 photos and illustrations. Cloth $12.00. $4.95 Paper.

BOOK OF SUCCESSFUL HOME PLANS. Published in cooperation with Home Planners, Inc.; designs by Richard B. Pollman. A collection of 226 outstanding home plans, plus information on standards and clearances as outlined in HUD's *Manual of Acceptable Practices.* 8½″x11″;192 pp; over 500 illustrations. $12.00 Cloth. $5.95 Paper.

HOW TO CUT YOUR ENERGY BILLS, Derven and Nichols. A homeowner's guide designed not for just the fix-it person, but for everyone. Instructions on how to save money and fuel in all areas—lighting, appliances, insulation, caulking, and much more. If it's on your utility bill, you'll find it here. 8½″x11″; 136 pp; over 200 photographs and illustrations. $5.95 Paper.

WALL COVERINGS AND DECORATION, Banov. Describes and evaluates different types of papers, fabrics, foils and vinyls, and paneling. Chapters on art selection, principles of design and color. Complete installation instructions for all materials. 8½″x11″; 136 pp; over 150 B-W and color photographs and illustrations. $12.00 Cloth. $5.95 Paper.

BOOK OF SUCCESSFUL PAINTING, Banov. Everything about painting any surface, inside or outside. Includes surface preparation, paint selection and application, problems, and color in decorating. "Before dipping brush into paint, a few hours spent with this authoritative guide could head off disaster." *Publishers Weekly.* 8½″x11″; 114 pp; over 150 B-W and color photographs and illustrations. $12.00 Cloth. $4.95 Paper.

BOOK OF SUCCESSFUL BATHROOMS, Schram. Complete guide to remodeling or decorating a bathroom to suit individual needs and tastes. Materials are recommended that have more than one function, need no periodic refinishing, and fit into different budgets. Complete installation instructions. 8½″x11″; 128 pp; over 200 B-W and color photographs. (Chosen by Interior Design, Woman's How-to, and Popular Science Book Clubs) $12.00 Cloth. $4.95 Paper.

TOTAL HOME PROTECTION, Miller. How to make your home burglarproof, fireproof, accidentproof, termiteproof, windproof, and lightningproof. With specific instructions and product recommendations. 8½″x11″; 124 pp; over 150 photographs and illustrations. (Chosen by McGraw-Hill's Architects Book Club) $12.00 Cloth. $4.95 Paper.

BOOK OF SUCCESSFUL SWIMMING POOLS, Derven and Nichols. Everything the present or would-be pool owner should know, from what kind of pool he can afford and site location, to construction, energy savings, accessories and maintenance and safety. 8½″x11″; over 250 B-W and color photographs and illustrations; 128 pp. $12.00 Cloth. $4.95 Paper.

FINDING & FIXING THE OLDER HOME, Schram. Tells how to check for tell-tale signs of damage when looking for homes and how to appraise and finance them. Points out the particular problems found in older homes, with instructions on how to remedy them. 8½″x11″; 160 pp; over 200 photographs and illustrations. $4.95 Paper.

SUCCESSFUL STUDIOS AND WORK CENTERS, Davidson. How and where to set up work centers at home for the proessional or amateur—for art projects, photography, sewing, woodworking, pottery and jewelry, or home office work. The author covers equipment, floor plans, basic light/plumbing/wiring requirements, and adds interviews with artists, photographers, and other professionals telling how they handled space and work problems. 8½″x11″; 144 pp; over 200 photographs and diagrams. $12.00 Cloth. $4.95 Paper.